To: Adria[n]

Life is a Journey...

Live Your Best Life ⚡

Thank you for joining
me on the Alphabet
Circle Journey

Dr. [signature]
8/21/19.

The Alphabet Circle Journey

LIVING YOUR BEST LIFE

Maxine Wright-Walters, Ph.D.

BALBOA.
PRESS

A DIVISION OF HAY HOUSE

Balboa Press books may be ordered through booksellers or by contacting:

Balboa Press
A Division of Hay House
1663 Liberty Drive
Bloomington, IN 47403
www.balboapress.com
1 (877) 407-4847

Print information available on the last page.

ISBN: 978-1-9822-0580-5 (sc)
ISBN: 978-1-9822-0579-9 (hc)
ISBN: 978-1-9822-0581-2 (e)

Library of Congress Control Number: 2018906643

Balboa Press rev. date: 10/05/2018

Table of Contents

Acknowledgment

My most profound gratitude to Dr. Thelma Francis for her Spiritual and Universal knowledge that brought clarity to my insight of understanding on a Higher level. Her knowledge of Universal truth gave me the breadth and depth of the ideas I needed to complete this work. Her laser-sharp comprehension of The Spiritual realm opened up unaltered pieces of my soul and gave me the view of a world I only imagined before working with her.

Preface

Sitting on the beach on a seemingly ordinary day observing the horizon and watching waves rolling into the shore, I had an awakening, allowing me to tap into what I have always been aware was inside of me. It was in the pause of this moment that I got inspired and led me to the writing of this book.

To my birthplace, the beautiful Island of Jamaica, I want to say thank you for the memories and adventure. To my friends who have stood by me during those times when I was so misunderstood, I want to say, "Thank you." To my siblings, thanks for being there with me on this journey. To Danny Sr., and my two boys Richard and Erik, thank you for the inspiration. To my parents, Eric and Ina, thanks for pouring so much of yourself into me. My papa, I thank you for all those beautiful moments on the farm with you. They have been the foundation of my experience as a Being who became aware. Thank you for teaching me that a little girl could dream big dreams. Thank you for sharing with me. My mama, I thank you for believing in me. Thanks for all the inspiring words.

Introduction

"What is the purpose of Life?" I asked. Growing up in my childhood, I was both puzzled and intrigued by life and death.

It made no sense to me that we were born to live, and then to die. I felt somewhere deep inside me that there was something more. I have been chasing this something more with the hope of finding it. Deep in my soul, I have been searching for the answers to this daunting question of life and life's purpose. From my view as a child, life could not be a blank slate; it made no sense to me that we were just born to live and to die.

As a child, I would sit in class and daydream. I was looking through the window and staring into acres and acres of prairies. In my mind's eye, I watched myself frolic on carpeted grasslands below the trees. Their rushing leaves sway to the rhythm of the island breeze, as the ninety-eight-degree temperature soothed my spirit. The sun appeared far in the sky, pointing its laser-sharp rays towards earth, forecasting a perfect island day. Unfortunately, I have never been in a classroom with such a window. It was not until I started on the quest for my "best life" that it dawned on me that those mental images were day visions. I would literally get out of my physical body and watch myself go to the vast spans of grasslands to romp and frolic. Those were such happy moments for me as I danced among the trees; my dress hem curled in the wind.

Poised intently in that scene, I would listen to the wind as she gusts through the trees in the distant hilltop. I looked and watched in awe, the first visible leaves dancing to her rhythm presenting a domino effect, transferring their motions from tree to tree. The wind sounded like laughter as it moved in my direction; the trees in her path caught the laugh too. Even in the ecstasy of this beautiful illusion, I could still see my classroom, the teacher, and the blackboard with the information written on it. I realized I could be in two places at the same time.

As a child, I loved the great outdoors and grew up on the island of Jamaica—what a combination! I had the best of both worlds. Island life provided many joyous intimate connections with nature, which formed the core of who I am.

The height of my day was my greatest joy when I could accompany my papa to the farm. I was always drawn to the farm. It was as if something was pulling on me to be in that setting. Those memories of walking with my papa to the farm have been indelibly printed on my mind. I must have been six years old. Our first stop on our way was always at the Breeze hill. Here papa would pause atop the hill, his hands holding his machete across the back of his neck. He would look at the crystal clear blue sea beyond us, punctuated by the reeds swaying back and forth with the froth bobbing in rhythm with the wave.

"Praise God!" He exclaimed. Taking a deep breath, releasing it and again he exclaimed, "Praise God! What a great God!" He continues. This praise was his adoration for the Creator. When he uttered those words, I always felt chills going through my body. I had an experience that I could not describe as a young child. But it was an experience that has been embedded in my soul as I grew up.

Being at the farm felt serene and natural. Papa and I were a team. Religiously, upon arrival, papa picked a bunch of jelly coconuts, so I could consume as much as I wanted of the delicious drink and jelly-like pulp. He was acutely aware of my great love for coconut water, and the ritual that went with the consummation of it. As I sat on the earth, he placed the chopped coconut in my hands so that I could drink its water. Afterward, he would cut the husk open exposing its beautiful jelly-like pulp so that I could consume it.

Sitting on the earth brought me peace and joy. Looking back at that time was a heavenly experience for me. We plowed the land and sowed seeds and sometimes made rows of dirt banks for our crops.

We then watched the position of the sun in the sky to tell time. When the sun was exactly overhead, it was noon. Our shadows were directly underneath our feet. It was time for lunch.

The cooking experience was a big part of our day on the farm. We gathered three big stones for the fireside, and wood from the residue of fallen trees. We were now ready to light a fire. Water was taken from a nearby drum that collected rainwater from the roof of the hut on the farm. Papa cooked (what my mama calls bush food), and we ate it from banana leaves, with the chop-sticks papa made from tree branches with his machete. This was the sweetest food to my taste buds. Not because my papa cooked it, but because it was cooked and eaten fresh from the earth in its native environment. The water came from the earth. The produce came from the earth on papa's farm. We cooked it on the earth. Then, we sat on the earth and ate the food. This connection with mother earth was a compelling experience in the scenery of my life.

Papa and I drove the cows to the waterhole to drink and then graze in various sections of the pasture. I would jump in the waterhole and frolic, splashing myself from head to toe, as my papa looked on smiling, and nodding his head with the approval of my joy. I just had to—I could not resist the water because it was calling my name.

During the "dry season" when there was little rain to fill the water holes, papa would hamper the donkey and put me on its back to ride to the storage tank to fetch water for the animals. This ride was exhilarating. I bounced up and down as the wind blew in my face, my hat swung to the side of my head with the constant gallop of the donkey.

I felt oneness with the animals, and it was as if we understood each other. They knew I loved being there in their home, and they consented to my presence with their voices singing, their sounds bouncing and rallying throughout the quietness of the landscape. The wide-open span of nature was calling my name. I had to respond. I had to go to greet and meet it. It was in the pause of those moments that some of my life questions were answered. I have never left behind, the smell of the freshness of being outdoors in a pristine environment.

I have always known that I was different. Different for me meant, I was destined to do non-normal things. It said for me that I marched to the beat of my drum. I was always at my best when I lived with no boundaries—a free spirit. And this was my farm experience with my papa. Looking back, I now realize that these experiences as a young girl were "a pouring into my spirit." Although at the time I had no clue, I was wide open to the experience and enjoyed every moment of it. Today, those experiences are like yesterday, and they are still so vivid in my mind.

I was always attracted to anything that has nature stamped over it, and I am still intrigued as I observe life "in all its elements." My observations, interactions, and attraction for nature and connecting the dots have brought me to the place of this book.

The Alphabet Circle is our life's journey from the letter A to Z. At birth, we get on this Alphabet Circle and start on our journey of experiencing life;

all kinds of relationships, and at some time after that, all of these relationships will exit the Circle. This exit will be at some letter between A and Z. Which one will it be? No one knows. How do we enjoy this journey on the Alphabet Circle and connect to every experience, even if at the moment we perceive it as "difficult?" How do we look at what we label as a negative experience, get the lesson and evolve from it? How do we embrace every interaction from a positive perspective, so that we can live our best lives? How do we live each day as the best life with ease and at peace? This book will answer these questions for us. Let's get started.

Chapter 1

Life is a Journey

It's now early in the morning. It is as early in life as your mind can recall. People who play an integral part on your life journey knowingly, or unknowingly surround you in your daily experiences. The questions are, what is the duration of these relationships, and which letters represent their end? As of now, no one knows. I suggest to you that they are all on the Alphabet Circle.

My friend Dave explained to me that he is a student of life, who is always open and willing to learn. But even a faithful student of life does not know where on the Alphabet Circle which relationships will be snuffed out and which will persist. Life as we know it is an unknown. Therefore, life is unknowable. What we know is what we have experienced. We do not know about the experiences we will have later, tomorrow or next week. Where on your Circle will these experiences start? Where on your Circle will these experiences end?

What is this Alphabet Circle? And how does it relate to my life? Consider your life as your experience. The Alphabet Circle is a best life concept. It is our life journey, and it is our footprint in the universe. The journey on this Circle goes from the letters A to Z. The letter A represents our birth or starting point on Earth, and the letter Z represents our physical body's exit from planet Earth. And then, there is that space between the letters Z and A. We have always existed as spirit energy before we took our human bodies. We lived in this space between the letters Z and A. This I will refer to as the soul level. The prophet Jeremiah writes, "I knew you before I formed you in your mother's womb" (Jeremiah 1:5, New Living Translation) and this is the space between the letters Z and A to complete your Circle. We resided in this space before having flesh bodies— the area of only soul activity and no flesh manifestation. This is the space in which you got all your raw materials and tools for maximum efficiency on the planet. This is where you were wonderfully and mightily made. The Circle is one directional and each person is on his or her Alphabet Circle. The time spent on or at each letter depends on the individual's experience, response, and whether or not he or she got the lesson.

The Alphabet Circle concept offers that we exist on this Circle at two levels: as a human being, which is the physical level, and as spirit, which I will call the soul. Similarly, there are two levels of interaction on the Alphabet Circle to complement the two levels of our existence. One interaction takes place at the physical level, and the other at the soul level.

The Alphabet Circle consists of twenty-six letters like the English alphabet. But with the Alphabet Circle concept, each letter represents a phase of life that you can and will experience.

As we travel on this Alphabet Circle, we encounter new and different relationships. We also might end some relationships. Some stay for a long time and others for a short time. The lessons that we learn from these relationships or interactions are for our souls' growth, and may not necessarily be for the human experience. But if we focus only on the human experience, we usually have pain when these interactions end. Relationships are formed due to the *soul-to-soul* bonds, which we will discuss later. Soul energy is released that contains information you need for that particular interaction and hence the journey.

On the Alphabet Circle, we create. Everything we build on the journey is a relationship and is manifested at the physical level. A relationship is described as a way in which two or more people or things are connected with or involve with each other. So every association can be viewed as a relationship.

Our life's journey can be likened unto many things, but there is one experience that captures it well. Standing on the reefs in the Caribbean Sea. If you are standing on a portion of the reefs where the water is about neck high, it is easy for the ocean's current to throw you off balance and move you off that rock. You must stand on rocks of the right height. Along with this, you have to stand with arms outstretched to balance yourself on this reef so that, regardless of the strength of the ocean's current you can stand. That's our life's journey. We must find an area in which to operate so that we are in balance, and learn the lessons we are supposed to, as we traverse this Alphabet Circle.

So, we wake up each morning and carry out our daily routines without thinking. We go off to school or work. We return home in the evening, eat dinner, maybe relax then get ready for bed. It's a process we will repeat tomorrow.

In our daily lives, we often overthink some things. Other times we do not think at all. But what if we think of every person and every encounter as being on our Alphabet Circle? What if we thought of every encounter as the meeting of souls who, upon gathering make a decision about; how they should coexist, for what reason, and that this is based on each soul's wants and needs?

Then, here comes "Monday morning quarterbacking." We put the "ole" brain tape recorder on and replay our past and argue what would have happened if we played the game of life another way. The result? We go through life hurt, wondering the reason for our losses, when in fact we should look for the lesson. Every one of those relationships was meant to end when it did. Can we embrace this? Ending an interaction does not mean that a particular relationship will never resurface. It can, and it may, as long as the souls find the need to come together again.

If we viewed each relationship or each interaction as finite, we would be more tolerant when its end arrives. We have been conditioned to see our relationships as being infinite. That is, they will last forever. So when a relationship ends, that is, it has arrived at its point on the Alphabet Circle where it ceases to exist. We are saddened and question its death or ending.

We live in a culture where we boast about how long we've been friends with others. We tend to gloat about long-term friendships, and sometimes we talk about them in such a way to suggest that we are stable and reliable. But does longevity in an association means you're stable? No. It says that the interactions on the soul level are still within their agreed-upon delivery of experience of spiritual growth.

Chapter 2

The Theory of the Alphabet Circle

With the Alphabet Circle concept, there is a dual existence. As a human being, you are having experience as a soul and also experience in a physical body.

On the Alphabet Circle, we have soul chemistry. That is, souls bond to form relationships, or to put it in layman terms, to deliver an experience. When souls bond—the bond formed is called the *soul-to-soul* bond and the process is called soul bonding. The strength of the *soul-to-soul* bond has nothing to do with how long the interaction or experience lasts but merely what tasks it will be required to carry out. Simply put, you need more energy to meet the lessons of the interaction consciously. It is through the challenges of the experience that souls grow more vibrant, stronger, and more beautiful. This means that, with each challenge we overcome, the energy of the soul becomes less dense, more refined, and closer to the Creator.

Energy is released when the *soul-to-soul* bonds are formed and also when they are broken. This is called soul energy. The soul energy field is packed with information useful at the human level, but we are not always conscious of it. The decoding of this energy field is critical for an enjoyable, exciting, and fulfilling journey on the Alphabet Circle.

So how does all this work? You have a desire or a need at either the conscious or unconscious level. When this happens, the souls are summoned. At their initial meeting, souls know why they were summoned and decide to address the desire or need they came together to fulfill. The souls know how long it should take to get the mission accomplished, but the physical being may not know because it is controlled by the ego. You see, the ego is that part of your consciousness in the physical reality that controls and dominates your physical experience. However, if your response to the interaction is not fulfilled from the souls' perspectives, then they may choose to stay longer.

How do these souls interact? How does it happen? Souls communicate through a process called bonding. In chemistry, we describe molecules as being made up of atoms. Atoms are the basic building blocks of the universe. It is everything we can see around us, and even the things we cannot see, such as the air we breathe. Atoms are minuscule. There are millions, billions or trillions in the tiniest speck you can see.

Atoms form bonds to create molecules through a process called bonding. Water is an example of a molecule. Bonding is the same concept as two persons developing a friendship. Remember, friendship is also an intentional interaction. The atoms form these bonds to become stable. Similarly, friendships are formed on the Alphabet Circle to help you on your journey and present the feeling of understanding, well-being, and balance. As with life, everything moves toward a state of equilibrium as the universe, which is energy, always shifts towards balance. The types of bonds that are formed in creating molecules depend on the kind of atoms. In the same way, you are attracted to certain folks with whom you interact or form friendships. The type of association depends on the needs and wants of the individuals creating a relationship. There are two ways in which molecules are formed; either by sharing electrons, which is similar to you sharing with your special person or by giving and receiving electrons, a process that happens simultaneously. This is similar to you meeting a friend for an activity.

Atoms are smart. In forming molecules, which is the sharing process, they have figured out that based on their makeup; it is better for them to share their electrons to become stable. In the giving and receiving of electrons, the atoms have figured out that it is better for them to either give away or accept electrons to become stable.

When the bond forms by sharing electrons, it is called covalent—a powerful bond. When the bond forms by giving and receiving electrons, it is called an ionic bond—a weaker bond.

This scientific explanation helps you to understand the concept of soul bonding. Some of the bonds or interactions formed by the souls are very strong or covalent, and some are not as strong or ionic. The bonds can be likened unto friendships you develop with various folks. Some of the associations are close that you may refer to the other person as your best friend. Others are seen as just friends. For example, your best friend bond would be your covalent or shared, and your "just friend" bond, would be your ionic, or charged bond.

So how does this concept work on the Alphabet Circle you may ask? When you have a desire and put it in the universe, whether through thought, or spoken word, you summon the experience you ask for, and souls show up to make it happen. This action takes place at the soul level. Be mindful of your thoughts about your desires because it is the thoughts you think that will manifest in your experience. Sometimes, you are not fully aware of your wishes, but know that the soul still responds on an impersonal level. On the Alphabet Circle, a desire is a desire whether or not, you are fully aware of your intention and motivation of that thought. Once the willingness gets into the universe, the souls always respond to give you the experience you ask. The souls then make a decision based on the want, need, and intended purpose to either coexist in a shared or charged fashion just as atoms in nature.

When *soul-to-soul* bonds are broken, coded data are released in their bond energies. This information is for you. These are the things you think and feel in your daily life. Why? When your *soul-to-soul* bond is broken, and the coded information is released, it is what skews your world in a relationship with other souls, especially if the data received has left you in a negative place. It can also be reflected in your personality and how you relate to others. That is why when you go back to resolve unfinished business in people's lives, it creates healing.

You must connect at the soul level to read and understand the encrypted messages. These messages are the lessons to be learned from the intention of your interaction. If you miss the lesson, the experience can and may repeat itself. If, and when the experience happens again, you get what is known as the déjà vu experience. In responding to these messages all along your Circle, you create your Impact map (I will discuss this further later), which will become more visible to you. This Impact map is a diagrammatic representation of your emotional responses to all your interactions on your Alphabet Circle, and hence on your life journey. When you review your Impact map, you can see more clearly your life's journey, and the lessons learned. When you examine your life experiences, you are looking at your Impact map.

On this journey, there are two levels of interaction—one at the physical level, and the other at the soul level. The physical level interaction happens in the head, which is where your ego operates. It is logical. On the other hand, the soul level connection is what you need to understand. You have moved to a level of consciousness where you let go of ego to bond at the soul level. Then, and only then, you can live your best life. The physical level interaction is not always in tune with the soul level and at times will react to what it thinks, hears, or feels without verification at the soul level. The soul level interaction comes with clarity and understanding and therefore peaceful relationships with one another rather than "rush to judgment," which is what the ego level gives you.

How then do we stand and be in balance, so we are not moved or washed away by life's daily currents? How do we decode all bond energy available to us and interpret them so that we can have the most fulfilling journey, and with the right interactions, and experiences? How do we bring awareness to our soul level interactions so we can benefit from them? How do we bring awareness to the physical level interactions? How do we provide a space where the two interactions coexist to maximize our life experiences so we can live our best lives? Let's delve into the phases of the Alphabet Circle and find out more.

Chapter 3

A is for Alright

In every phase of your life, the letter A is the beginning. This is the Alright phase on the Alphabet Circle. In this phase, everything seems fresh and new with some amount of excitement. When you are in this phase in your Alphabet Circle journey, you have a definite sense of hopefulness. You are now in the marathon of your life journey. Now, each of us is running this marathon, but at a different speed. And as with a marathon in the physical world, there are people along the race-path that are there to give you support in different ways. Some are there to cheer you on, while others are there to provide you with water and replenish your nutrients, and this is Alright. Your journey will be filled with highs and lows. The people you meet in this phase seem genuine, and your thoughts may be that they will be on this journey with you to the letter Z or the physical end. Little do you know that individuals in some relationships may only get to that phase where the souls understand that the lesson from the experience is learned. This may be to a letter other than Z. The feeling of genuineness comes from souls being in sync, deciphering your message maps, and this is Alright.

In this phase, I want you to know and focus on the fact that:

All
Life
Relationships *can*
Initiate
Good
Human
Thoughts

And this is so whether you are aware at the physical level or not. However, the soul will respond to these thoughts and give you the feeling of the thought and the experience, and this is Alright.

The Alright phase is a birth phase wherein everything seems to be and feels Alright. Remember birth brings newness and that's what is happening in this phase. Some of the raw materials that you were given to come to the planet are manifested in this phase, and it is Alright. You can think of it as a halo effect, as the innocence of the interactions is not dissected, just absorbed. In other words, they are not questioned, only accepted. In this phase of the journey, encounters feel new and fresh. There is a lot of hope, which is stimulated by the excitement generated by the newness of the interactions. The newness creates for you, lots of stories in the mind as imagination is at its peak. There is a lot of creativity of the mind of how things will be as the brain activity heightens, all concerning your expectation. You have the hope that longevity is in play for your journey, your ideas, your career, and or your relationships. Be aware that this is your default, so that you are open to other results.

Think of the Alright phase as similar to your first meeting the love of your life and how exhilarating it feels. You get so excited that you start to see a long-term relationship and possibly, you going to the altar. Yes, you create ideas in your mind of how you think the relationship will go, and this is because of its newness, your hopefulness, and the anticipated unknown path. This too is Alright.

This is also the blossoming phase. You may have sown seeds in all kinds of grounds that you consider to be Alright. These grounds can be friendships, jobs, a particular project, or family. You plant these seeds because within you, there are feelings that something will blossom and bear fruits. These feelings can be both at the conscious and sub-conscious levels. It really does not matter where they are, as your actions will do the work.

You feel an authentic power as it radiates from inside. You have a particular paradigm, which seems to be in sync and will always work for you. You are convinced at this stage that everything is Alright, and for you—it is.

This is also the foundation and entrance phase on the Alphabet Circle life journey. Some interactions will enter your Circle at other points, which will be the foundation phase for those persons, relationships, or events. This means that the Alright phase can take place anywhere on this Alphabet Circle, and its duration will be person specific. This is a beautiful phase and similar to our foundation phase in life when we first learn to read. Similarly, we start on the Alphabet Circle with sounds, then letters, and then, we can sound out words. Next, the most beautiful thing happens. We can read and form sentences. Yes, we can now communicate with words. Yes, we now have a language. Yes, we can express what we are feeling, what we are seeing, and what we are hearing. We are enlightened and aware of all that is around us. Some of us may become absorbed in it, while others may not. It depends on our perspective. This awareness brings excitement to this stage, and it is Alright.

Dreams begin and it's Alright!

New plans begin and it's Alright!

New perspective begins and it's Alright!

Eagerness begins and it's Alright!

Hopefulness begins and it's Alright!

With these new beginnings, you think that this is perfection in this phase. Your experiences all seem to be in alignment. All is in order with the natural order of things—the natural order of the universe.

So what's happening here? The *soul-to-soul* bonds are formed and energy is released within you. At the human level, you are tapped into this soul bond energy, and this is what brings about this feeling of being Alright. You are connected with the soul level in such a way that you decipher the codes released in the soul bond energy. You are now in tune, which gives you the presence of Alright.

None of the relationships formed in the Alphabet Circle is guaranteed. We have all met that one guy, or girl with whom we believed we were going to have a lasting relationship because of the connection we felt in this Alright phase. For me, this was my ex-husband. We met in college and were able to finish each other's sentences. We ebbed and flowed. It was as though we were soul mates. We had so many great experiences together; that no one we knew thought that we'd end up being apart. But it happened. Relationships are not guaranteed! Being a soul mate does not mean you have to be in an intimate relationship with someone for the duration of a lifetime. And, if you do have this close soul mate relationship, it may not last forever.

(Bullard, 2012), a licensed Marriage and Family Therapist describes it in this way "Soul mates are brought into your life so that you can grow and expand into the best version of yourself" (para. 3). Be aware that from these interactions you will grow into the best version of you.

It's essential that we nurture and grow the interactions formed in this Alright phase. The care needed to do this is no different than when we plant seeds into the ground. Within the seed, there are all kinds of prospective plants and fruits. Know that there is power in the seed as it brings forth plants and fruits of all sizes, shapes, textures, and colors. Similarly, within your interactions on the Alphabet Circle, there are friendships of all kinds, sorts, and duration.

How do we make sure our seeds grow? In life, we first prepare the soil and make sure that nourishment is there. If for some reason we determine that enough nutrient is not present, then we add fertilizer to the earth. This is part of the process to ensure that our seeds will grow. On the Alphabet Circle, this is the same as learning someone else's love language, so you can be a caring friend to that person. Next, we create a hole in the ground so it can receive the seeds, which must be then cared for and watered. In all but a few days, Mother Earth has worked her magic, and transformed the seeds into sprouts and then plants. This is the birth phase, and it's Alright.

As the plants bursts out of the ground, the warmth of the sunlight pours down on them. Similarly, on the Alphabet Circle, you speak active words that come to life as great events or relationships. This is Alright! To keep these plants growing to maturity, we must water them because anything that is not watered or nurtured will die. This goes for every relationship on your Alphabet Circle. They must be cared for in order to thrive. This means that you must invest in your relationships on your Circle. Your investment includes your time.

As these plants grow, we must remove the weeds from around them, so they are not stifled. Weeds grow fast and are always attracted to what we have willfully planted. In my own garden, I clear weeds at least once per week, so they do not overrun my vegetables. You too will need to be aware, and pay attention to the weeds that show up in your relationships. Also, figure out how often you will need to clear the weeds on your Alphabet Circle to keep your relationships growing. It could be once per week, or once per month; make a note of this schedule, so you will not forget.

Weeds on the Alphabet Circle journey are specific. That is, what may be a weed on your journey may be a needed plant on someone else's journey. So it is in this phase for you, and it's Alright.

Here are some things we need to know about this weed prevention stage.

We are the farmers of this journey, and it's Alright!

We must create a space within which our relationships can survive just like the garden.

We must keep weeding around our interactions so that they can thrive.

We must tend to our relationships so they can come bursting out of the Alphabet Circle with excitement as we pour our energy into every one of them.

Every relationship is Alright!

Every relationship is supposed to be there.

Every relationship is there for a specific reason, and if we stay aware, we will connect the dots because the universe speaks.

Let's revisit the weeds for a moment. Why? Left unnoticed they may overrun your space and hence your life. They can be the "takeover mama" or the "tenant from hell" who is so hard to evict. Notice that the weeds are distractions to your intended interactions. These weeds represent stuff that's on your Circle that you must take notice of and eradicate immediately. Sometimes, the weeds seem to blend in from afar, but as you take a closer look, you will see that they are masking as intended interactions. This is the same for many things on your Alphabet Circle that invade your space without an invitation—some of them blend in well. Weeds can even be persons you believe to be friends, but they are not!

There are all kinds of weeds. Some are deathly dangerous, in that they will seriously harm your physical and mental health. Case in point—the poison ivy. It will take over the host on which it thrives. It looks quite attractive and blends in well with other plants. However, for some, once you encounter this weed, there is a severe reaction, and you may need medical treatment. Know when you have weeds like the poison ivy. To the unaware, it seems like a willful plant. Getting rid of the poison ivy requires care.

You must know how to do so without contaminating or harming yourself. On the Alphabet Circle weeds can be places, persons or things. Be on the alert to their presence. To enjoy this phase of the journey, you must identify your weeds, and remove them without contaminating yourself. What are the weeds on your Alphabet Circle? What are the intended interactions they are trying to overrun?

During this Alright phase, there is peace, and there is a presence. You are connected to your interactions because they are new, and the air of curiosity is healthy. The newness of it all allows you to show up, and be present because you're in the Alright phase. As you read this book, ask yourself, "Where am I on my Alphabet Circle?"

Chapter 4

B is to Breathe

The letter B represents the Breathe phase on the Alphabet Circle. Breathe as you travel on this journey called life. Life will give you the experiences you need; not the experiences you want. Spiritually, you say God knows what you need. And this God is the Creator. The Breathe phase will happen again and again on your Circle because there is always the entrance and exit of persons, relationships, jobs and so on. All of which are experiences on this life journey.

In the Breathe phase, here is what I want you to do. Take long deep breaths and B- R- E-A-T-H-E:

Believe

Relationships

Enter *the*

Alphabet Circle

To

Help *you*

Endure

In this phase, you are still fresh with ideas as you are not far from the Alright phase, which is filled with hopefulness. I want you to BREATHE. You are alive and need to bask in the experience. Every experience on the Alphabet Circle is useful, so pay attention.

Some of the relationships you developed during the Alright phase you may have now lost. That is, some of the souls that entered on the Alright phase have already exited your journey. They have stepped off your Alphabet Circle and have walked onto someone else's, who needs an experience. They are committing again to a finite spiritual experience with a new soul and hence, a different human being. However, you are still fighting the challenge of the experience. For example, Jackie rented an apartment. She paid a month's rent and did not pay rent for the next three months. This posed a challenge for both Jackie and her landlord. They had both entered into a relationship based on trust, which Jackie broke and caused her landlord not only financial pain but also physical and emotional pain. This situation resulted in turmoil between them that severed their relationship.

Although this was a business transaction, there are lessons to learn. So we can see here, that there are different lessons for both of them to learn from the same situation. Not all transactions have to be emotionally embroiled. These interactions can take place with different people in our lives, but they can cause pain, and we need to become more aware of the process in the challenge of the experience. This is why it is essential to Breathe, so you do not get embroiled in the emotional pain of the experience, but focus on the lesson and Breathe.

Don't use energy to chase interactions that don't end well. The souls have stopped those transactions because their season came to an end. They have moved on. Are you accepting that? Of course, you would like one more chance to see if you can resurrect a broken friendship. But I will tell you to save the energy and use it for some other connection. Just Breathe.

Breathe and focus on the breath. The importance of focusing on the breath helps you to stay in the moment, being present with your situation. So concentrate and Breathe.

Breathe, and remember, what we focus on is what we bring into the experience. Know that there is no new creation. The great scholar King Solomon writes,

"There is nothing new under the sun" (Ecclesiastes 1:9, New King James Version). This is really what it is. Although you believe, that at the human level you are creating something new, you are merely bringing awareness to something that already exists in creation. Breathe as you think about this. Like energy, that can neither be created nor destroyed; our souls are nothing but energy fields. We cannot create new ones. We use the ones that are there, as we move along the journey to create new experiences—life. At the soul level, there is connecting, disconnecting and reconnecting. Hence, on the Alphabet Circle, you do not look back to regain experiences or relationships. Your role on this journey, and particularly in this phase is to B-R-E-A-T-H-E.

The Alphabet Circle is non-sequential, in that any phase can occur at any time to get you the desired experience. It does not rewind. It does not go backward. No one knows which experience will show up next. That is the uniqueness of this Circle. You believe what you want to believe about the duration of a job or a friendship, based on some feeling deep within you. It is called a journey because as you become aware, you are supposed to let things flow in their natural order and Breathe. Breathe deep and hard as you embrace your experiences. They will all come to you. You don't need to rush out to get them. Be present, and it will happen. It will happen at the opportune moment. Breathe, be present, and allow yourself to experience each interaction, and take away the lesson you need to learn.

If you ever sit at the ocean's edge on a calm day and watch the waves, you will notice that in the deep, the waves move to one rhythm, and in the shallow, toward the shore, they move to another rhythm. At this more shallow point, the waves rise a bit higher and move into the shoreline with a soft swoosh. Notice the togetherness of the waves even as they move through different depths of the ocean. Notice also, that the waves roll in one direction, and that is toward the shore, same as our path on the Alphabet Circle—one directional.

We are connected to our experiences, and our responses are proportional to the interactions when we Breathe and are in sync. The proportionality can be a direct relationship or an inverse relationship. What does this mean? It means that in our direct relationship, our responses get bolder as our interactions increase. In the inverse relationship, the opposite happens. Our responses get demure as our interactions increase. We must Breathe, and take note of our responses.

Breathe as the leaves do in the wind. They find their rhythm no matter how strong the wind, and they dance to the music of this breeze. We too must Breathe, and dance to the rhythm of our experiences. Breathe and listen. What is the beat of the interaction? Which chord is being played? What is the cadence of the interaction? We need to know because we must find the rhythm of our journey, and dance like the leaves do. All around us we see examples of just going with the flow. We need to learn to go with the flow.

You need to Breathe deep, long, and slow to absorb the ebb and flow of your journey. Some of you adsorb, which is taking on a superficial coating, and not being fully immersed in the experience. Don't do that! Take deep breaths to lessen the emotional toll that this journey may have on you. Close your eyes as you Breathe, and believe that those who are with you at this point are supposed to be in the experience. Those who are no longer on your Alphabet Circle have learned the lesson. This means, those who have left are supposed to, because the lesson of experience for that portion of their journey was learned. Look at it this way. When each one learns the lesson, he or she must move on.

Breathe, and be open to receive new experiences from your interactions as you inhale and exhale. New souls are showing up for you all the time. These new souls will create for you, the specific environment that you need to ebb and flow on your journey's ride. Remember, each soul knows perfectly well what it needs, and the experience will be provided through the interaction. Now trust and believe then B-R-E-A-T-H-E!

Chapter 5

C is to Create

Create what you want on this journey. This is your right, and you possess the ability to do so. Create the life you envision for yourself. And, because you can do this, you are now able to order your days. You can now dictate how you will react. To Create is to dictate. It's like programming an arrow to go north. When the arrow is released from your hands, it will only go north. There must be an awareness of what you want to Create, and where you want to go.

You have your desires, and now, you must Create them. This means, you can manifest what you want, through your creative mind. Sandra, my friend, expressed she had a sincere desire to be a nurse. She felt that if she could become a nurse, her life would become everything she wanted. In talking with her, I learned that this had been at least a twenty-year desire.

"What have you done about it," I asked.

"Nothing. There is just so much going on in my life right now, and I don't have the money," Sandra responded.

"OK, that's fine let's start at the beginning. What do you think you need to make this nurse stuff real?" I asked.

"Money. Go to school . . ."

"Great! You could start at the community college. It is not expensive to go there, and you may be able to get financial aid," I offered.

"But, I don't have my GED," Sandra countered.

"Did you tell me this is a lifelong dream, and you do believe it will change your life?" I asked.

"Yes! That has been my dream since I was a little girl."

"Great," I responded. "Then how about you creating that dream now? It is your dream, and you have the power to Create it. You are the only one stopping yourself right now."

After a long pause, Sandra remarked, "I think you are right, but where do I start?"

"So you should start here—get your GED. Then, you can go on to the community college, and possibly a four-year college. Girl, the sky is the limit." I encouraged.

Within a few months, Sandra completed her GED, and she registered in the nursing program at the local community college. Today, Sandra has a Masters' Degree in Nursing because she finally created an environment for her twenty-year desire to manifest.

Sometimes, you need to let someone else know about the desires you have been carrying around in your mind. Tell someone about the unrealized dreams and potentials inside you. In speaking about them, your words start to Create the environment for them to manifest. Don't take your unrealized dreams and possibilities to the grave. Your dreams and talents will enhance your journey and the world. Know that when you are in this space of lifelong desires, or dreams, you are withholding your skills and talents from the world. In essence, you are cheating the world of your skills and abilities. Don't rob the universe of your contribution.

Some of your desires, you are immediately aware of because they are at the physical level. Others, you are not consciously aware of as they are at the subconscious level. But immediate awareness, or not, you find yourself being pulled in a particular direction.

When I started to explore my best life journey, it was because I had a pull and a push. I felt an emptiness inside me, but a yearning for something more, that I couldn't quite put my finger on. I thought I was being called to something higher. I could not go through a day without these ideas coming to me. I had no peace until I made a conscious decision to follow the pull and push. And, here we are on this Alphabet Circle. Always investigate the pull and push, as there is some desire you have that wants you to Create a space for it to be realized.

Even as you are creating, new souls are attaching to your Circle, making new interactions. But some souls will make a finite connection and will be with you to the end of the experience. What will it take to connect to such a soul? What will it take to attract such a soul?

In the Create phase, you are and feel empowered. Your life seems to be going well. Everything is falling into place. You are making the right connections. Life, as you know it, is excellent. Some of the interactions in the Alright and Breathe phases may be lost here.

However, new connections are gained. At the soul level, souls who show up in this phase know why they are here. That is, to get your desires to manifest. The souls will carry out their assigned activities to the agreed upon phase or stage, and when the assignment is completed, they exit that role. Be a gracious host, and allow these relationships to bear fruits at the physical level by being consciously aware.

Create! Create! And Create some more! You can Create the life you desire! Know, that your desire is in alignment with your purpose. What does that mean? It means that your desires are there to fulfill parts of the elements of your journey. You have these particular desires, and they are pieces of the puzzle of your life journey. Once the pieces of the puzzle are filled in, the created desire is completed. That is why you must Create your desires. Be deliberate and precise in the process.

You are reading this book, and your question is, "How do I go about doing this creating stuff? How do I Create this happiness?" It is a decision you make every day you wake up and must continuously remind yourself throughout your day. Decide that, you are going to be happy no matter what happens. This is called the happiness decision. Once it is created within you, and you act on it, it spills over into your environment. It is very infectious and becomes visible. People will notice that you are happy. Some will even comment on your exuding happiness.

Create the environment for happiness. You must shrug off each event that sets out to railroad your happiness decision. Think of positive things. Surround yourself with positive people. In your mind Create beautiful sceneries and places. Remember you are the creator of this scene. You are the author of this happiness. You are the author of your story.

You can Create the future you want. When it manifests, it shall become your present. You are responsible for that future. You are responsible for the stories in your journey. If you Create the environment of failure, then failure is what you had in your mind. Create the stories you want to manifest. You are responsible for your happiness. Create the happiness you desire. You are responsible for your success. Create the path to your success. Create whatever you would like it to be—success or failure, happy or sad. Know that only you have the power to do this, and no one can stop you when you choose to Create.

You may be thinking someone or something can make you happy. You believe that, if you get that next job or college degree, it is going to change your life, and make you happy. However, no one can make you happy, only you. You must Create your happiness from within. Others may bring you situational happiness.

But as soon as the stimulus is removed, the happiness is gone.

Growing up as a child, I was always told by my parents that the sky was the limit, and I could be anything I wanted to be. This was ingrained in my mind that I could not think of anything, nor did I believe there was anything that I could not do. This mindset gave me such confidence growing up, and always caused me to search out the "How can I achieve this?" It starts in our minds through our thoughts. Create a new mindset where you believe that, you can Create the story you would like for your journey. Create the mindset that we all have creative juices flowing, and you will use yours. Create what you need for your interactions, not for anyone else. "So how do I get this mindset?" You ask. Self-talk. I want you to keep telling yourself that you can Create whatever you want in your space. I suggest you start doing this self-talk in front of the mirror, so you can see your whole physical body while you put both it and your mind on notice about your new mindset. While you are doing this, pay attention to what's going on around you before your desire is manifested. Remember, I told you earlier that souls respond to your desires and give you the experience of those desires. This new mindset is what Creates the new experience.

What kind of life do you want? What kind of job do you want? What kind of mate do you want? What kind of friendships do you want? Are you equipped with what it takes to Create your new story? *The Introduction to the DISC Behavioral Analysis, Your guide to understanding why people do what they do*, describes DISC as personality types (The Institute for Motivational Living, Inc., 2011). It describes:

D being the Dominant personality and there are only 3% of them in the population. They are dominant, decisive, goal-oriented and the leadership type. The

I personality is instinctive, influencing, inspirational, and they make up 11% of the population. The S personality is stable, steady and secure, and they make up 69% of the population. The C personalities are correct, calculating and creative, and they make up 17% of the population (p.7).

The Behavioral Analysis lists Hereditary, Role Models (up to age 12) and Experiences (after age 8) as the contributing factors to behavioral style (The Institute for Motivational Living, Inc., 2011). This contributes to the differences in people. "People are different, but they are predictably different" (The Institute for Motivational Living, Inc., 2011). What this teaches is that our behaviors are different depending on our situational experience. However, a lot of what we do is predicated on our experiences. It also teaches that all "Behavior styles are modifiable" (The Institute for Motivational Living, Inc., 2011). No one is stuck with just one particular kind of behavior. We are all a combination of some sort of this DISC, and no one is stuck with just being an all D or I or S or C.

So how does this play into the Alphabet Circle? On the Alphabet Circle, you know you are the creator of your experiences, and yes, you are equipped to do so. What you Create is finite. What you Create on your Circle will exist until its purpose is accomplished, and this could happen at the letter where it was Created or at any other letter on the Alphabet Circle. You do not know which letter this will be. However, what you know is that it will happen. You can, therefore, be prepared that when the mission is accomplished, then that interaction ends, and it is okay. Your takeaway is, you are the creator of your experience. This is how you Create the experience you want to fulfill your life!

Chapter 6

D is for Details

Pay attention to Details. It is said, "The devil is in the Details." The universe reports, pay attention. Life reports, pay attention. This is sometimes called connecting the dots. If you spend the time to observe your surroundings, your friendships and your relationships, you will notice how they are honestly doing. On the Alphabet Circle, Details are essential.

In paying attention, you will become aware and start connecting what you are feeling, and hearing at the soul level with what you are experiencing at the physical level. You will notice which souls are attaching as well as which souls are detaching, and which souls are exiting your Circle. All are manifested in what physically comes and goes from your life. These physical manifestations could be jobs, friendships, careers, etc. Know that:

Details

Encourage

Tolerance

Awareness *and*

Intention *of*

Life

Souls

Let the Details steer you to think about your *soul-to-soul* bonds. What is the information present in the soul bond energy, and how is it interpreted? How is it manifested at the physical level? As you focus on the Details phase of the journey, ask yourself, how aware are you? Are you feeling lack, or are you feeling satisfied? Are you feeling fear, or are you feeling secure? Are you feeling helpless, or are you feeling empowered? Check in at the soul level because the Details are all around you.

It is said that when Mother Nature is about to do something drastic (drastic from the human perspective) like a flood or a Tsunami, animals that are on low lying lands move to higher grounds. This has been described in a report *Listen to the Animals: Why did so many animals escape December's tsunami?* (Sheldrake, 2005), He writes:

> Many animals escaped the great Asian tsunami on Boxing Day, 2004. Elephants in Sri Lanka and Sumatra moved to high ground before the giant waves struck; they did the same in Thailand, trumpeting before they did so. According to a villager in Bang Koey, Thailand, a herd of buffalo was grazing by the beach

when they suddenly lifted their heads and looked out to sea, ears standing upright. They turned and stampeded up the hill, followed by bewildered villagers, whose lives were thereby saved. At Ao Sane beach, near Phuket, dogs ran up to the hill tops, and at Galle in Sri Lanka, dog owners were puzzled by the fact that their animals refused to go for their usual morning walk on the beach. In Cuddalore District in South India, buffaloes, goats and dogs escaped, and so did a nesting colony of flamingos that flew to higher ground. In the Andaman Islands stone age tribal groups moved away from the coast before the disaster, alerted by the behavior of animals (para.1).

Why is this so? The universe reports and the animals pay attention to the Details. However, often times, most humans who are within the vicinity of those animals are caught in the disaster. Why? Most humans rarely pay attention to Details in nature. As described by (Sheldrake, 2005), the people in his piece did not notice that the animals had moved to higher ground. The Details were there, but those present in that location failed to see them.

Farmers typically can tell you a lot about Mother Nature because they observe her every day for years. They learn to read her messages, her nuisances. Why is this so for farmers? Farmers are special kinds of people when it comes to Mother Nature. They have great respect for her as they pay attention to the Details in her messages, and they know that Mother Nature is never wrong. They watch her daily sending out her messages, and they interpret them for their optimum benefit. I saw this in my father. Each day he would read what Mother Nature forecasted so he could be prepared on his farm. For example, he knew when to expect a storm and would move his penned animals out of harm's way. Farmers know their livelihoods depend on Mother Nature. They are interacting with her each day because they need to know optimal conditions for growing their crops or raising their animals. When you interact with Mother Nature as much as they do, you acquire a deep understanding and respect for her. Simply, farmers come to understand a lot more about nature than the average person who would have no reason to know signs and seasons. So is life on the Alphabet Circle. It is like a farmer intimately interacting with Mother Nature. In the same way, you must pay attention to Details on your Alphabet Circle so that you know when to get optimal conditions for your crops. Your crops are your interactions or relationships on your Circle.

Pay attention to the Details that are all around you. They are the guiding posts for your life. Missing Details can take you off course, and sometimes cause a collision as signals are jammed, or completely missed allowing chaotic situations on your journey. Pay attention, and you will see that the Details answer many of your questions. Details are footprints that, if followed, will lead to places where you are destined to be. This can be a physical or mental place.

Pay attention to the Details of your inner energy. Messages are entwined in these energy fields, which your soul sends to you in your feeling. Pay attention to the equilibrium of the *soul-to-soul* bond. Pay attention to when these *soul-to-soul* bonds break, and there is a shifting of soul bond energy. Remember, souls break their *soul-to-soul* bonds to exit that experience on the Alphabet Circle. In so doing, they expel energies within which are encoded messages with Details for you. These Details are manifested at the human level, as relationships or interactions until they exit the Circle. Pay attention to the Details of the encrypted messages, validate your feelings in the moment, and go with the flow.

Pay attention to the Details of your desires. Sometimes you need to ask yourself, "What is the real reason for this desire?" At times you have unrealized dreams, hopes or desires, or it might be the feeling of shame and guilt that's preventing you from achieving your goals. But whatever it is, the important thing is to explore what's blocking you from achieving your desired goals. Look at the Details. When we dissect the Details, we may no longer want that desire. Klifton was an acquaintance who had a strong desire to be married. See, he was newly divorced from his high school sweetheart and was cautioned not to rush to get remarried. Klifton referred to himself as an "alley cat" and mentioned that he needed to have a woman in his home. He would forego dating and get right to marriage, and that he did. The new marriage lasted less than six months. In exploring his desire to be married, I learned that he was raised in a foster home with no one ever showing him love. He was lacking, and yearning for a mother's love and thought that to have a wife would fill that need. It did not happen for Klifton. He had not paid attention to the Details of his desire to be married and could have saved himself the pain inflicted upon him and his new wife. Because of his unawareness, he did not pay attention. Although he went to counseling and was told how to address his deficiency with his mother, he did not follow that advice. He did not realize his dream to have the ideal wife was due to his unresolved relationship with his mother. Details are important on this Circle, so pay attention.

Pay attention to the Details of your interactions. Sometimes all that glitters is not gold. I met Dave, and we clicked immediately. He seemed like a nice guy. Our conversations were profound. They ebbed and flowed. We both talked about becoming the best versions of ourselves. At the physical level, Dave was up to no good. He was the kind of man who wanted to take advantage of women. But at the soul level, I was able to see the bleed through of the intention of his soul's desires, but he was not aware of it. After every conversation with Dave, I got insights at a deeper level, but he was not aware as his intention was from the ego. He became a catalyst for this work. My relationship with Dave helped me to see things from the soul level. It provided insights from which I needed to grow and learn. On the physical level, people can be misled by the relationships they enter, so pay attention to the Details from the soul level.

Chapter 7

E is for Earth

The Alphabet Circle represents the Earth on which our lives and experiences are built. We walk upon the earth, sit upon it and plant seeds into its core. We are always in intimate contact with the earth, except for being airborne. In the same way, we are in close contact with our Alphabet Circle. It is our playground.

The earth supports life, which supports people. For example, the earth supports plants and animals that are food and a necessity for people. Similarly, the soul interactions support our desires and the people we need on the Circle. The journey supports relationships that are important for your experience on your Alphabet Circle. These relationships will support all the interactions that you need to live your life in the present. These relationships are even applicable to your pets. New experiences and situations are being created while some are ending. Consider the Alphabet Circle as "The Earth" where all your needed provisions are available for a fruitful life. Note that, fruitful is different for everyone. Make sure you understand what fruitful means for you. For some, it may mean having children, while for others, it may mean having the right job, being married or having a home. Only you know what is fruitful for you, and typically you strive toward that. One of my friends in high school wanted to be married and have children immediately after graduation. For her, that was fruitfulness. She had no interest in going to college or pursuing an education beyond high school. Interestingly, the classes that she liked and excelled in were those that had something to do with her fruitfulness. Cookery, needlework, and dressmaking were a few of the things she liked to do. Teachers would encourage her to try other interests and career goals. But, she would only listen to them to be polite. This girl knew what fruitfulness meant for her, and she rejected all the advice that did not line up with what she wanted to do. She got married right out of high school and started her family immediately. Today, she is still married with five children and is very happy with her life. She achieved fruitfulness— her fruitfulness. Pause and consider this. What is fruitfulness for you, and are you on a path to achieve it?

Just as the earth provides all things vital to the existence of all human beings, so too this Earth phase offers all things needed for your life journey within your Alphabet Circle. Just as much as the earth bears fruit, so does your Alphabet Circle. Just as plants flourish on the earth so too can relationships, ideas or jobs thrive on your Alphabet Circle. Just as the rain waters the earth, you need to have rain to water this Earth phase of your Alphabet Circle. This rain shows up in various forms. You have to do some things within your power, to prepare for the rain on your Circle. Rain falls on the earth from moisture that accumulates in the clouds. When the moisture content reaches a certain percentage, for reasons beyond the scope of this book, the clouds burst open, and the rain pours down on the earth. You have to create, the atmosphere on your Circle to cause a certain percentage of moisture to be absorbed so that it can rain on your Circle. Your job is to cultivate rain-attracting conditions. How much of this rain you will consume depends on your location on the Circle, and how receptive you are for this rain to pour upon you. Rain on your Circle is what we sometimes call blessings.

Your interactions or relationships are the things that create rain on your Circle. However, the conditions must be right for this to happen. It is no different than fruits, which must bear in their correct season. After the right conditions are cultivated, they encourage pollination, blossoms, and then, fruits.

As you work and play on the Earth, take note of the many things that it provides. Notice the mountains, the undulating hills, the beautiful grasslands, the valleys, the craters, and so on. All these things are represented on your Alphabet Circle. Some relationships or interactions represent those mountains, or undulating hills, or grasslands. When you encounter these points on your Alphabet Circle, you get a similar energy as you get when you experience them on the earth. So, if it's a peaceful feeling in your encounter on the mountain on earth, so will it be when your mountain interaction occurs on the Alphabet Circle. At your soul level, you have a pre-recorded response to these points. Therefore, when the experience shows up on your Circle, your default response will appear.

For example, an undulating hill experience is one that is always up and down but does not last for a long time in either the up or down phase. In my thirties, I met Luna, an older woman. I was a young mother, newly divorced when she came into my life at what seemed to be the right time. We shared the same Jamaican culture, and I thought that was good for me. I knew no other Jamaicans in my community at the time. My experience with Luna was likened to the undulating hills. As soon as one chaotic episode was finished, she had another one going. They did not last very long, and in my experience with her, she was most excitable at the up phase of each episode. Looking back, I reacted just the same way I did as a young child walking over many undulating hills in Jamaica. I embraced the experience and anticipated the next wave.

The Earth phase is centering. Think of it as an attachment, and an encounter with all who are on your

Circle. *Soul-to-soul* bonds are being formed to get you an experience. *Soul-to-soul* bonds are being broken after accomplishing the experience. The journey is long, and long here is relative, but you are sustained by the relationships you have created along the way. Even the ones that have ended have played vital roles in shaping you to answer your call and living your life purpose. What does this mean for you? How do you know you are living your life purpose? You will know when you are at peace with what you are doing. You find fun in doing it. It will not feel like a chore. You are typically drawn to the things that are part of your divine purpose, and they come easily and naturally.

Be mindful that the Earth is resilient. It endures, and it embraces. It's been around for as long as humans have existed, and it embraces all life on it. Notice that the earth's gravitational pull does not decide one day not to embrace certain folks, and you see them flying in the air. This does not happen. The earth exhibits warmth and a favorable environment for nourishment and growth of many things. So are you on your journey. You can do the same thing as the earth in your Earth phase. You must endure on the Circle, and embrace all your experiences as they come to you. You can nurture and provide an environment for growth, by deep focus, and be receptive while being able to absorb that which is necessary, positive, sustainable, and vital for you on your journey. You will have to decide what falls into these categories, so you must never lose attention.

Within this Earth phase, there can be a "rocking of your world." Just as the rain comes down and it waters the earth, giving rise to great things like flowers and fruits. On the other hand, there can be such a downpour of rain that it causes a flood. So it is, on your Circle. In your Earth phase, your rain can bring you beautiful things that bring you excitement, enhance your life, and cause you to grow. Like a new relationship, it allows you to explore activities that are new and exciting. You try them and continue to do them because you like them. On the other hand, your rain can give rise to floods, which might be an Earth-rocking moment on your Circle. It is not a matter of if, they will happen, but when, they will happen.

One Thanksgiving Holiday, my husband and our two sons went to New York to visit my in-laws. It was our baby's first Thanksgiving and a fantastic trip. I returned home with a high from my trip to a devastating Earth-rocking moment, when I got news that my beloved brother who was visiting South Africa was stabbed and killed. It was as if a volcano had erupted in my life. I cried for years. Today, although I have not gotten over my grief, I have learned to manage my feelings when they show up. You too can learn to control your emotions that show up after an Earth rocking moment in your life.

Just as the earth recovers from a flood, you too will have a recovering from the floods in your life.

After a few months, I accepted that my brother was gone and never coming back. That was my recovery. Just as a landslide sometimes stops with the help of nature or man, you too must stop an avalanche on your journey. My brother's passing was a landslide for me, and so to cope, I visited with my spiritual advisor often, where I was able to discuss my feelings. I spent long hours connecting with the Creator, and that helped me to heal. Sometimes, you may have to get the help of someone else such as a doctor, a minister or a counselor. Know the difference; do not get a lawyer if you need a doctor. You need to know your story or symptoms so that you can get the right help. Be mindful that sometimes you need a helping hand. Seek it. Remember, the Earth phase supports all provisions necessary for a fruitful life.

Chapter 8

F is for Finite

Everything on the Alphabet Circle is Finite. This means that every interaction, and therefore each relationship, has a predetermined end date attached to it. However, no one knows its duration. Don't be fixated on the idea that there is a specific duration; just remember that there is one. With this thought, embrace every interaction. Show up, be fully present, and enjoy, but do recognize that the interaction is not eternal.

The idea of finiteness allows you to focus on the now, the moment, and to bask in the interaction. Feel your energy levels soar, and your happiness bubbles up from within you. You are now in unison at both the human and soul level. You are in the ebb and flow of your Alphabet Circle. The journey is being enjoyed, and you can't wait for the next chapter, as life is lived chapters. When one closes, another opens.

The finiteness of each interaction on the Alphabet Circle brings acceptance to a new level. Knowing that every relationship is Finite opens the door for a willingness to accept what is. Acceptance allows you not to overthink, but let the experience show up for you, and when it ends, you are content that you got what you needed out of it knowingly or unknowingly. Acceptance takes your focus from the behavior or the reaction of others to being on yourself. Why is this? You are not responsible for other people's behavior. You cannot dictate what they will do. However, what you can control is the way you react. Helen was a long time friend. She had experienced a lot of changes in her life that clearly impacted her in a negative way. These manifestations showed up as fear, rage, and anger. It was almost impossible to partake in any activity with her, without her exploding for one reason or another. As her friend, I cautioned about these behaviors, how I received them, and the negative impact they had on me. After a year of experiencing these interactions with her, I realized their impact left me drained and exhausted, to the point where I would be poised to attack once I felt her rage and anger. When I realized how her negative energy was affecting me, I came to the point where there was nothing more for me to learn from this type of experience. Hence, I terminated the relationship. The *soul-to-soul* bonds were broken, and my Finite relationship with Helen had run its course.

What I learned from this experience is that I alone can control my actions and reaction. This applies to the way you react to any experience on your Alphabet Circle. Be in control, the interaction is Finite and will come to an end. You do not know how soon, but you know that it will end. Remind yourself that your experiences are not infinite, and do not project what you would like it to be. If you do that, you will set yourself up for disappointment and miss the lesson. Pay attention to the lesson!

Why are relationships and experiences so Finite? Remember, souls, come together in response to a desire. When two souls have a desire, they come together in the physical world to experience the lesson. In the human experience, they may not be aware that there are lessons to be learned and that a specified time is attached to the experience. However, the souls know. This is no different than when you sign a contract with someone to do a particular job; you have the desire to get a job done, and the contractor also has a desire to do the job for you. When the lessons from the experience are learned, the *soul-to-soul* bonds are broken, the relationships end and they leave that point on your Alphabet Circle. Be aware that each letter on the Alphabet Circle is Finite, and so is the experience!

When you arrived in the earthly experience, you became Finite on the Alphabet Circle. Hence, you are only here for a Finite period. We do not consciously know when that end will come. But the soul knows. Is there anything infinite on the Alphabet Circle?

Think of it as a pregnancy. The baby will be born when it's ready, regardless of the date the doctors give you for the birth. For that baby, when the state of readiness arrives, the time is now! There isn't anything you can do to stop the delivery process at this point. So too, are the interactions on the Alphabet Circle. They proceed or stop when it's necessary.

Do not allow fear to come upon you because of the awareness of a Finite experience. For many of us, when we are aware that something will end, we get into our sports cars, fasten our seatbelts and drive ourselves right into the fear zone. Why? Why, do we respond this way? We are trying to manipulate the results in our minds. We are trying to forecast a picture of what the journey will be like when a particular interaction ends. This is going ahead of the interaction, moving into a future that does not exist. At this point, it is only a figment of our imagination, yet we think about the outcome and immediately experience fear. Know that there isn't anything to be fearful about, but when the experience happens; it is a Finite experience. We need to open ourselves up to the present and be more aware of the lesson from the interaction.

Some of the Finite experiences will and can have a crippling effect, due to the emotional pain, caused by our lack of awareness of the reason for the experience. Seek out ways of what you need to learn from the lessons of the experience. When you get the lesson, you will grow from it. One experience is the emotion of fear. It is a Finite emotion, based on, how you interpret the events of an experience. That emotion may appear again and again, depending on how you are interpreting each experience in different situations. So hence a person may experience feelings of fear or joy, based on how that individual understands the event that creates the feeling, which is real for him or her. For those of you who have had a FEAR experience, you know exactly what I mean by this.

In August 2008, my ex-husband and I took our two kids on vacation to Disney World. While there, I rode the "Tower of Terror." If you have been on this ride, you know that it is an elevator of some sorts that drops down thirteen floors, and this may happen three or four times by random selection. Our particular ride dropped four times. I was so scared when the elevator got to the top of the structure and what seemed like we were way up in the heavens. The ride opened its roof or top window, so we could get a good peek at the outside to remind us of our location. We were looking at the top of trees and mountains, so the mind was very aware that we were way "high in the sky." Then the window closed and the elevator dropped again and again! When I got off this ride, my life was never the same!

I started experiencing a fear that was crippling because of this traumatizing experience. Through the next few years, this fear followed me, uninvited. However, my emotional reaction to this experience caused me to fear heights, fear bridges and fear mountains for a long time. Roads that I once drove on without thinking suddenly became a problem for me to navigate, as my uninvited guest "fear" reminded me that my car was running off the road. I could not drive over bridges without my palms sweating. I no longer enjoyed one of my hobbies—driving. I was miserable. I was aware and searched for ways to deal with this new uninvited guest. I wanted and needed to get rid of fear. I knew the emotion was Finite and needed to hasten it to its demise.

In frustration, I started sharing my experience with my friends. I asked if anyone else was having the same difficulty. Part of me wanted to believe it had something to do with the aging process. I had just turned 40 years old. Then one day, telling one of my girlfriends what I was going through something happened. This particular friend, knew I loved driving and had logged hundreds of thousands of miles on the road driving. She was taken aback. After listening intently to my story, she said to me, "That is not of God!" This registered with me, and I became immediately aware that my feeling of fear was an emotional reaction to my experience of that "Tower of Terror" ride. She retorted, "You need to pray through that." It was my "Ah Ha" moment. Something in me woke up, and I realized I had to look at this uninvited guest, fear, differently. Most importantly, fear is Finite. I needed to become aware to eradicate the feeling of fear from my life by reinterpreting the events of my experience—false expectation appearing real. I followed this strategy of reinterpretation, and four years later I was over it! Yes, the fear experience was Finite, and it ended.

Know that there is always room to overcome your experiences because they are Finite. You do so, by being aware of the lesson from the experience. Do not allow the experiences of your Finite interactions to bring uninvited emotions to you. Be aware! Live in the moment of awareness! And pay attention to the lesson to Live your Best Life.

Chapter 9

G is for Geography

Are you in the right location? Are you in the right place? Are you where you are supposed to be? Did you respond to the right situations, so that you could get to the right place? Not only did you respond to the right situation, but also, did you do so appropriately and adequately? Have you charted the correct path? Your Geography is most important. You must be in the right place where souls can connect. This means the right place physically, mentally, and emotionally. You can only receive what you are supposed to on your Circle if you are ready, and your location service is turned on.

If you are not on the right wavelength, you will never get the signal. Why? You are on a different wavelength than the signal being transmitted. So what does that mean for you? On the correct wavelength, you feel peace. You feel in order. You feel connected. You must be aware of your position, or place at all times, and your connection to your wavelength. If you are listening to an AM radio station and the information you need is being transmitted on FM radio, it is unlikely that you will hear that information, because you are not tuned to the right channel.

On the Alphabet Circle, any letter could represent this wavelength. Awareness brings your geographical location from the satellite to your receiver, so someone can see where you are located. This means your location is always known, and there is a clear path to you. What emotions are you experiencing when this happens? You have peace, and calmness in your spirit, and you know in what direction you need to go. It could be North, South, East or West.

Think of your Geographical Positioning System (GPS) you have on your phone. If you turn off the location service on your GPS application and you enter your destination address, when you ask it to take you there, it will not. The GPS, as smart as it is, will not function without a preprogrammed map system and its location service turned on. If you pay attention, you will notice the map system on your GPS may use a different route to a particular location, than the map system on another person's GPS. It is like the saying, "Every clock is minding its own business." Well, your experience on your journey may be slightly different depending on whether you are using a Yahoo or a Google map system on your GPS. They will both get you to the address or location, but one may take the scenic route, and the other the local road. Or, you may take longer to arrive with one than the other. It is the same principle on the Alphabet Circle. Everyone's journey will not be the same, but you will get to your destinations. With the GPS, you may preprogram it to use non-toll roads, local roads or highways, as it takes you to your destination. This destination has a longitudinal and latitudinal point. Thus it's specific. Similarly, you can preprogram your journey on the Alphabet Circle. This may be done by bringing awareness to your experience. Allow the experience to come to you, and bring you the lesson. The souls will take care of the rest.

On the Geography phase of the Alphabet Circle, you must pay attention, and make sure your location service is turned on. That is, you are aware. You must also know which map system is preprogrammed in your GPS. This means that, you must pay attention at all times, and make mental notes. Remember that the universe reports, so you will feel some familiarity, or peace if you are paying attention, and taking mental notes. Don't panic, you will find your destination with the GPS, but the experiences to get there are not going to be the same as someone else's. How many times have you been warned by a friend not to do something because of what could happen, if you do that particular thing? You end up doing it, but you have a different experience. Yes, because you are the author of your life, and some of us are better crafters than others. Therefore, don't use someone else's experience to judge what experience you will have. You are unique, and so are your interactions and experiences. In another way, how many things did your parents try to save you from, but you went ahead and did them anyway? That's because you must encounter your own experiences. Someone telling you about his or her experience does not mean that you will have the same experience. At the human level, there is a part of you that must defy what you were told, because you believe in your own soul's experience from the similar event.

On the other hand, if you thought that your experience was going to be the same as your parents, you would have done nothing, but accept their advice. To not accept is to go out and do it your way.

As an avid traveler, I always query a physical map no matter where I am going, because I want to have a physical sense of the landmass around me, and the general direction I need to travel. In other words, I don't want to navigate in the dark. I always view the topography, as this is important in terms of time spent on a particular roadway. The distance by a specific route may be shorter, but because of the terrain in which the road is built, it may take a longer time to travel the shorter distance. For example, roads with a lot of curves and hills tend to take longer to travel than a straight road on a flat surface. On the Alphabet Circle, you should query your map system, which is your soul, and get an understanding of the depth of and what it may take to resolve your situation.

You must also point yourself in the correct direction. That is if you want to go true north, or to the North Pole, you cannot be heading to the South Pole, or in southerly direction thinking you will end up North. That is not going to happen. Again, you must want to know where you are, and where you want to go. It is your job to know where your compass is pointing. You cannot "just give a blind eye" to your direction. Many will say, "I am okay with not knowing." The problem with that is, you don't have a specific direction that complements how you want to travel on your Circle. It is indeed a Circle, but you may be pointed in a different direction depending on where you are. What direction are you facing? You need to know so that you can make your next move.

Who are you? Do you know the Geography of your soul? Do you like to take the highways, or do you want to take the scenic route? This is important to know, to program your GPS since your best journey will be the one that complements the Geography of your soul.

Chapter 10

H is for Happiness

Happiness is a state of mind. It is also one phase on the Alphabet Circle. Earlier in the Create phase, I asked you to Create an environment to be happy. Now! Commit to be happy in the Happiness phase, regardless of your experience. Each day you get up, decide to be happy, whether or not you can see the sun from your location. Know that the sun is always there, whether or not you can see it. Don't limit yourself to only what you can see from your location.

Happiness is a decision that comes from within. In this phase of the journey, I want you to close your eyes, and look deep within. There is so much Happiness energy within you that can excite and swell. This Happiness energy inside you moves from potential energy to kinetic energy. This means that, it goes from a low level (due to its position) to a high level (due to its motion). You can think of it as the difference between sitting down and running.

As your days roll on, events take place, and you get experiences. Look at them and say, "I need them." The universe returns what we think into it. This really works. As the event happens, take a long deep breath and tell yourself, "I must be present." Each time when you lose focus, remind yourself by saying, "Be present." And stay present. You will notice that, you are better able to deal with your interactions and your experiences.

What do the experts say about Happiness? Psychologists Ed (Diener & Biswas-Diener, 2008) concluded, "Happiness is a process, not a place" (p.

9). According to (Seligman, 2002), "Happiness is not a competition. Authentic happiness derives from raising the bar for yourself, not rating yourself against others" (p. 14).

(Khoddam) Describes it this way, "A 'happy person' experiences the spectrum of emotions just like anybody else, but the frequency by which they experience the negative ones may differ. It could be that 'happy people' don't experience as much negative emotion because they process it differently or they may find meaning in a way others have not" (para. 2).

When you decide to be happy, "All hell will break loose." (See the Create phase). When you make a deliberate Happiness decision, almost always something may happen that might throw you off your Happiness balance. If this happens, shrug it off, and get back on your Happiness balance. There is so much Happiness energy hidden inside of you that, you can use it in every experience, and still have enough left over.

Do understand that when you decide to be happy, you are going to be tested. You may even delve into the unhappy zone for a minute. That too is okay, but get right back on your Happiness scale. Your Happiness scale allows you to fluctuate your levels of Happiness. In the fluctuations, you may be happier one moment, and less happy another minute. However, it is vital to maintaining your Happiness balance regardless of what state you are in. Eventually, with practice, you will become more aware of the Happiness within you. Let the positive energy within you rise, and remind yourself that you are choosing to be happy. With practice, your physical self will align with the soul, and you will be able to sustain your Happiness balance. It is like training your muscle to run a race. The more you practice, the better you become.

Have you ever been in love and felt that hopelessly romantic Happiness? You can feel this way all the time with a conscious effort on the Happiness scale. This feeling on the Alphabet Circle is based on your perspective. How do you view life? How do you see your experiences? Are you embracing your experiences knowing that you need them? Know that nothing happens in a vacuum? All relationships and experiences are connected.

How do you travel on the Alphabet Circle and maximize this Happiness? Sometimes, upon making your deliberate Happiness decision, you go to work, and it is that day, your boss decides to call you into his office to discuss something you did that he is not happy about. Instead of a discussion, he throws a tirade. Oh well, "If something can go wrong, it will go wrong." What do you do when things go wrong? Look at the positive. The universe has provided you with an opportunity for you to practice what you have decided to do. So, you Breathe deeply, center your thoughts, and remind yourself, you choose to be happy. Your boss' tirade has nothing to do with you, because your Happiness has penetrated and uplifted you to a place of balance.

One of the ways to be deliberate about your Happiness is to use the theory of a Quality Control program. Quality control is a set of procedures intended to ensure that a product or service adheres to a designed set of quality criteria or meets the requirements of the customer. One of the things that must be done within this program is a needs assessment or Gap Analysis. On the Alphabet Circle, this assessment is the Happiness Gap Analysis. A Gap analysis is an assessment of where you are now, and where you want to go, and what will it take to get you there. Be true to yourself in this process. Be honest. First, you assess your current level of Happiness and believe that for you, it could be high or low, because there is always room for improvement, to bring you into a place of your Happiness balance, which is a state of equilibrium. From this place of balance, there is a level of Happiness that is always maintained. So, now we know where you want to be. You have measured as you do in a proper quality control process. This level will be different for each person on the Alphabet Circle. Your Happiness Gap is the space between where you are right now, and where you would like to be regarding your Happiness. In paying attention to your space, you may recognize that there is a struggle to reach your desired level of Happiness. Struggle, suggests your life is not in sync, or in balance with what you want to accomplish. To fill this Happiness Gap, you must now make the adjustments to achieve balance. Remember, you are the only one who can and have determined what will make you happy. You continue to measure and correct, until you feel that you are in sync or in balance. This may take some time. There is no limit on when it should happen. Keep working at it until it's accomplished.

Mahatma Gandhi said, "Happiness is when what you think, what you say, and what you do are in harmony" [as cited in (Michelli, 1998)]. Can you relate this to your journey? If what you are thinking, saying and doing is not in sync, then you are not in a state of Happiness balance. However, all is not lost. You keep working on it, and with practice, it will eventually be synchronized. As humans, sometimes we say all the right things, but our thoughts, words, and actions are not in alignment. When your thoughts, words, and actions are not alignment, your Happiness balance is out of sync. Pay attention to your to your thoughts, your words, and your deeds to regain your Happiness balance!

Chapter 11

I is for Impact

There are Impacts to being on your Alphabet Circle. An Impact is an influence or effect. This is the phase where your experiences are diagrammed based on your emotional responses. Are you making the right connections? You have events happening in your life, and there are Impacts from these events. Have you connected the dots? Are you paying attention to the interactions and subsequent Impacts? A friend of mine told me, that his daughter was a perfect child until her last year in high school. At which time, as he described it, "She became a thug." He said, he was baffled by her behavior, and could not understand its source. Upon discussion, he revealed that he divorced her mother, that same year. That is, during his daughter's final year of high school. He described his child as a swim team champion, top of her class, very scholarly, and very friendly. He lamented that this child and her siblings were raised in a middle-class neighborhood, and they all exhibited what he described as, normal behaviors until this particular daughter began to demonstrate "thug-like behaviors." My friend did not connect the series of dramatic events that led to his divorce, and the subsequent Impact of those events on his child's behavior.

No Impact exists in a vacuum. All are manifestations of events that are acted out in behavior. Some behaviors are described as, positive and others as negative. The description of positive, or harmful behaviors depends on one's interpretation of his or her experience. I am not saying you are to become a psychologist, but you must pay attention to the Impacts of your experiences, and hence their manifestations on your journey. Take the time to observe your experiences and their demonstrations. This means, review how they are showing up in your life on your Alphabet Circle. And ask yourself, "What experiences are these Impacts coming from?"

There are many Impacts on your Circle. Start writing things down. Clues are left by souls who come and go in different phases on your Alphabet Circle. They leave tracks, and if you follow these tracks, they will lead you to your Impacts, and "Ah ha" moments. Your reaction to events is always, as a result of some previous experience that Impacted you positively, or negatively on your journey. Step back from your emotion, and allow yourself to see the situation for what it is. Your experiences typically dictate how you view your journey. But, no matter what the event, you can make a decision whether the experience is positive or negative; you will focus on how it Impacts you.

What are some of the Impacts of the relationships you have formed? What are some of the Impacts from the jobs you've had? Why do you think you have the job you currently have? How do these thoughts impact you? Remember, you are where you are supposed to be in your journey on this Alphabet Circle called life. What if you embrace the Impact, and understand that it was created from the experience from your desire, and the souls presented it?

Let's look at this another way. What is the Impact of living in your neighborhood? What is the Impact of having the neighbors you have? Who are the people on the journey with you at this time? Who are the people who were on the journey with you, but are no longer here? How have they Impacted your life? Can you see the reasons, or at least one reason for them being there, or not there? Do you imagine their presence to be finite? Every Impact is essential, whether you view it as positive, or negative. There are no negative experiences. You may be uncomfortable with an experience, but it is never negative, as life gives you only the experiences you need, and at the perfect time. You may not think the time of an experience is right, but the souls know better. When the experience shows up, focus on the lesson. Observe the Impact of the experience, or interaction. Connect all your Impact dots, and you will see your journey in full view. You have just created your Impact map. You will now look at the reasons for these interactions. As you review your Impact map, think about what are some of the Impacts of the *soul-to-soul* bonds? What are the Impacts of souls entering and leaving at different phases on your Alphabet Circle? What are the Impacts of souls bonding? What is the Impact of the full energy release from such bonding? You have lots of Impacts to review. You have lots of ways to view your journey and assess it. Now, ask yourself, are you satisfied with your Impact map? Remember, you control the shape of the Impact map with your reaction to the experiences on your journey. Make every effort to Create a map that will satisfy you.

Chapter 12

J is for Jockey

You are the Jockey on your Alphabet Circle, which is your life's journey. You dictate how this race will be run. Just like a Jockey in real life, you have a strategy and a plan for this race, based on your experiences so far, and the experiences you would like to have on your Alphabet Circle journey. You are in tune with your *soul-to-soul* bonds, and receiving a download, or deposit from them, so you can strategize on the Alphabet Circle. Being a Jockey requires discipline and preparation. It requires a commitment to perform this job. As the Jockey, you have to be in the right weight class to ride your horse. In a nutshell, a Jockey is a leader of his horse, which is his tool to run, and win the race.

Know that you are equipped to be this Jockey. You have what it takes. All that you need to be the Jockey is already planted within you long before you came to this planet. You may not be aware of this at the human level, but certainly, at the soul level, you are aware. When the soul level and the human level connect, the complete you become aware. This is the authentic you in a wave-like form in the crest and troughs of life; you are in sync.

A Jockey selects a horse that is suitable for his weight class. So too, you must choose your battles on the Alphabet Circle. Try not to win the battle and lose the war. Make choices that are suitable for you. This means, you have a feeling of peace within you about the choices you make. Be aware of your decisions on the Alphabet Circle. Know your weight so that you can choose the right horse for your weight class. Then, with the right strategy, you can win this race, on the journey called life.

You must take the best care of your horse on this journey. You must do this by being aware of all conditions around you, so you can keep it safe. You must also be aware of the circumstances, or situations that are not best for you and your horse and steer away from them.

By being aware you will Jockey your position on your journey. What this means, is that you will create the best situation possible. You will realize that sometimes, it's about intellect, and other times it's about instincts. Know when to choose either. Intellect will be most useful at the human level, and instinct will manifest at the soul level. Jockey yourself to the right choices. It's your journey.

Chapter 13

K is for King

The Alphabet Circle is your kingdom, which makes you King, (King here is gender neutral). As you know, the King makes all decisions in the kingdom, and he takes care of his subjects. Everyone you meet on your Alphabet Circle is in your kingdom and your subject. This means that, all relationships are in your kingdom. Take care of them. I want you to reign all over your Alphabet Circle. Walk all over your Circle and claim it. You are King of your domain. Be present. Show up for all interactions, and all relationships. Do not overthink it, and do not re-live the past. The past is the past and gone forever. It cannot be re-lived, so don't try.

(Google) describes the definition of a King as: *"Ruler of an independent state, especially one who inherits the position by right of birth."*

"A person or thing regarded as the finest or most important in their sphere or group."

"The most important chess piece, of which each player has one, which the opponent has to checkmate in order to win. The king can move in any direction, including diagonally, to any adjacent square that is not attacked by an opponent's piece or pawn."

Some synonyms of King are: ruler, sovereign, monarch, supreme ruler, crowned head, majesty, Crown, head of state, royal personage, emperor, prince, potentate, overlord, liege lord, lord, leader or chief.

All these descriptions refer to you over your Alphabet Circle. You are the chess piece! You are powerful! You are strong! You are King! So, be the

King! Be responsible for what you do, and honor your word, as the King does in the kingdom. You must rise above all odds, as King of the kingdom. As King, you must hear the unheard. To do this, you must be fully present at the soul level, so that you are in your highest self. Within the kingdom, all subjects work together for the good of the kingdom. So it is, on your Alphabet Circle. All interactions, both at the soul and at the physical level are for your good. Remember the universe will give you only the experiences that you need to get your lesson.

As King, you will make all the decisions in your kingdom, which is your Alphabet Circle. However, the King seeks advice from his advisors. So too, you will need to seek guidance in making some decisions, and choices on your Alphabet Circle. These choices will lead you down designated paths. Be wise with your choices. Seek advice when needed. Never hesitate to ask. Also, always ask the universe first. Remember, the universe returns what we think into it.

As King on this journey you must know when to delegate. Don't be overburdened with all chores. There will be many loyal staff, and confidants that you can rely on to assist you, as you carry out your duties in your kingdom. So it is on the journey of your Alphabet Circle. Do not overburden yourself, delegate!

The position of King is mighty. It makes you a leader; the leader of your life, your journey, on your Alphabet Circle. Although, you have a *soul-to-soul* interaction with someone else simultaneously on the Alphabet Circle, know that each one is King of his or her Circle. So each must take responsibility for his or her behavior in the experience. The *soul-to-soul* bonds know your position as King. So they offer you all you need to be King in your domain. Look inwards, and feel the powerful energy of your Kingship. Find solace in this.

Although you are King of your kingdom, be aware that at times, you will find yourself in situations where you will have to step back, assess, and possibly offer an apology. Know, that the King is never too mighty to apologize. At times, as King, you will have to offer forgiveness. Be open, and willing to do so. Know that the King is human, and experiences the human level interactions. Be focused. Know that your human level interactions are always connected to your soul level interactions so that you can perform at your highest level. As King, you must pay attention to your messages, which are in your *soul-to-soul* interactions. You are King in your journey on your Alphabet Circle.

Chapter 14

L is for Love

Love is a tender emotion. Love yourself first. Show Love in every relationship on this journey. What is this Love? The Bible describes it as; "Love suffers long and is kind, Love is pure, Love does not envy; Love does not parade itself, is not puffed up: Love does not behave rudely; does not seek its own; is not provoked; thinks no evil; believes all things; bears all things; hopes all things, endures all things. Love never fails" (1st Corinthian 13:4-8, The New King James Version).

A Course in Miracles (Schucman, 2012) makes a profound statement, "Your task is not to seek love, but merely to seek and find all the barriers within yourself built against it" (p. 404 Chapter 16 V: 6). In so doing Love will find you. You do not need to seek it; allow yourself to be open so that you can feel the flow of Love. Think of a moment when you felt so loved. Do you remember that feeling? Do you remember how excited you got? Yes, in the center of your being you have this Love energy, which you can activate. You do not need to depend on someone else's Love. Love is a natural emotion we experience.

Your relationships and interactions on this journey must be viewed from the place of Love. Some interactions are mild and some are deep. Love flows from all directions. Can you feel it? If we live from the level of the true self, we are living in Love.

The Love energy is in your heart, and you can feel Love anytime by focusing on this energy. (Gibran, 1923) writes in *The Prophet*, "Love has no desire other than to fulfill itself" (p. 2). You are

Love—Love embodies you. All along the journey, you have experienced Love. Can you remember a few of those moments? When you sat and had coffee with a long time friend, you felt Love. When you took a walk barefooted in the sand on the beach with a friend, you felt Loved. There are relationships you developed along the journey and immediately felt Love in those relationships. If you paid attention, there was Love oozing off those interactions, if you had awareness. You must be able to recognize this Love when it appears. As *A Course in Miracle*s (Schucman, 2012) pointed out, you must find all the barriers blocking Love. Once they are located and removed, you will feel the full effect of Love. Barriers can be anything in your life that is not in sync with your ebb and flow. It could be an emotion. It could be a person. It could be a relationship. It could be a ritual. It could be a god. It could be a thing. It could be a job. It could be a chore. It could be a past time. Take the time to observe, and you will find these barriers to Love that are loafing on your Circle.

In your state of Love, you readily forgive. You make no judgments. You make no assumptions. You "give the benefit of the doubt." When you are practicing this Love, some will accuse you of being stupid. Love is kind. Love knows no wrong. Say a kind word always—that is Love. Make loving gestures of kindness, and compassion that are expressions of your true self. In this state of Love, you have moved away from caring what folks think of you. You are in a space where you are aware of whom you are, and so you don't have to prove anything to others. You don't need to drive a particular car or live in a particular house. You are in the state of Love, so whatever car you drive or whatever house you live in, you will do so in Love.

Remember, Love knows no wrong. Always forgive on the Alphabet Circle. Forgiveness is for you. Not for the offender. When you forgive, you release yourself from any ill feeling that you may have harbored. This state of Love allows you to see the glass half full, and with this attitude; you will conquer mountains on your journey. In fact, you could overcome them all. Each, of course, will be conquered in a different time frame, and, or in different moments, but you will conquer. Ninety percent of it is your mindset, and ten percent your actions. Your mode in this state is, "I can do all things through Christ who strengthens me" (Philippians 4:13, New King James Version). This is what Christ and many scholars of Light have taught. Christ is Love. Christ represents Love—boundless energies of Love. If you activate the Love energy center within your heart, you can accomplish whatever you want. The universe will give you your desires, because you are open and receptive. Once you have a willingness to receive, the universe will deliver. Think of this as pouring water onto a dry sponge. That sponge will absorb water until it can absorb no more. It is drenched. Be that sponge so the Universal Love can pour into you.

On the journey, you must show Love, and you must receive Love. Love is everywhere. You don't have to chase it. The creation around you is Love. The souls coming and going on your journey are Love. The *soul-to-soul* bonds formed are Love. If you focus on your heart, you can feel the Love. You need Love to make this journey work for you. Through Love, you will enjoy some beautiful experiences. Love teaches you acceptance, and because you are accepting that you exist in a space where pure Love exudes, you are glowing. Your eyes are bright. You are in tune with the universe.

Chapter 15

M is for Motive

What is your divine purpose? Your divine purpose is doing what you were meant to do in your journey on your Alphabet Circle. Your divine purpose also depends on your Motives, and intentions of what you want to do, and achieve for your life. You arrived on the planet fully equipped with all the characteristics you need to do what you are supposed to do.

Years ago when I moved to Pittsburgh, I met a friend, Sandra. We both had small children, and we spent lots of time together so that both our sons could share playtime. I was always impressed with the way she interacted with children. It came so naturally for her, and children always gravitated towards her. I would see her come alive when she was in the presence of children, and I believe I can say she loves everyone's child.

Sandra completed her Masters' degree and was looking for her dream job. She wanted to work as an Ambassador to North Africa. This was not happening for her. One day, in discussion with her, I suggested that she might want to find work that involved children because I could see that was where she shined. She was dumbfounded when I made that suggestion and became very upset. She felt insulted by my suggestion because her Master's degree was in Policy on North Africa, and her dream was to work as an Ambassador in North Africa. She did not see her educational achievement on par with what I had said. I apologized that she felt upset, and consoled her by letting her know that I sensed her destiny and her purpose was to work with children. At that point, she recognized that my intention was not to insult her, but to let her see that she had a natural gift for working with children.

Fifteen years later. She had moved to a new city, became a high school teacher, and one day while I was visiting with her, she shared with me that she wanted to thank me. Sandra told me that becoming a teacher was one of the best things that happened to her. She was thoroughly enjoying her work with children. She said she was thankful that I was bold enough to suggest that fifteen years earlier. She further stated that, although she was furious by my suggestion at that time, "You were right!" Sometimes, it takes someone else to help you to connect the dots. That is why other people are on the Alphabet Circle with you. They can help you to maximize your potential. Sandra could have opted not to follow through on her divine purpose, but she did and found fulfillment in her work with children. Know when to follow through to meet your divine purpose.

Your Motive is to pay attention, careful attention. Canvases are laid out, and sceneries are drawn all around you. Beautiful colors are being painted that reflect who you are on your journey. Pay attention to the colors you see. What do they mean for you? Understand that everything has a meaning. Look within, for the wisdom of it all. Dots are being placed all over your Alphabet Circle. These dots are to be connected. The answers are there and have always been there. It is for you to connect, interpret, and understand them all. Your Motive is to communicate with your *soul-to-soul* bonds so that you can find all the answers you need.

Sometimes the *soul-to-soul* bonds do not end, but they become loose enough to allow each one to go off to pursue his or her life purpose. The *soul-to-soul* bonds remain peripherally, while the souls go off to pursue their own goals.

From as early as six years old, my father told my youngest sister Mindy that she would become a lawyer. As a young child, she was precocious with a big vocabulary that could only have belonged to a grown up. My father in his wisdom connected the dots. He planted the seed, and Mindy received and believed it. So much so, that in high school she completed only courses that pertained to law, and did not worry about the others. Mindy became a lawyer at the young age of twenty-three, and she is still practicing today, and enjoying her life's purpose. Your Motive is to believe in your destiny and to act upon it.

What is your Motive on your Alphabet Circle journey?

Your Motive is to be your highest self.

Your Motive is to complete your journey in a fashion that is pleasing to you, the author of your life.

Your Motive is to be diligent with the experiences, in your journey.

Your Motive is to know when to let go.

Your Motive is not to chase relationships or experiences.

Your Motive is to be present in your space and receive the answers to fulfill your life's purpose.

Your Motive is to liberate yourself from negative emotions.

Your Motive is to stay focused, and positive.

Your Motive is to listen.

With deliberate creation as your focus, your Motive is to be present at all times enjoying the now moment—you are actively participating, and basking in the present moment, and the now. How exhilarating!

Your Motive is to have the right mindset, which is, a winners' mindset. (Milton, 1991), in the poem, *Paradise Lost*, said this about mindset:

The mind is its own place and

In itself

Can make a Heaven of Hell, a

Hell of Heaven

You will build your life according to your mindset. The Bible, in the Book of Exodus, tells us how the Children of Israel in Egypt were freed from slavery. With freedom in hand, they crossed the Red Sea and got to the Wilderness. However, even after such a miraculous journey, they were stuck in the Wilderness for forty years. Partly, because of a slavery mindset that plagued them. They became a Nation in Egypt in slavery, and so they had a slavery mindset. This was very difficult for them to overcome even though they had witnessed all sorts of miracles. The Bible says that when Moses sent twelve spies to the Promised Land, only two, Joshua and Caleb came back, and said they could go there. The other ten came back and reported that they could not go there because the land was filled with giants. Joshua and Caleb had the mindset of "we are able," but it was the minority view. It was two out of twelve, only a sixteen percent view. The other mindset was that of weakness or a defeatist mentality. That is, they saw problems through their weaknesses. But the majority view was "we are not able," and because of this mindset, the Children of Israel stayed in the Wilderness for forty years. It was not until the death of Moses forty years later, when Caleb and Joshua became the leaders of the group, that the once minority mindset that kept them in the Wilderness became the majority mindset. The new leaders executed in the "we are able" mindset and led the Children of Israel out of the Wilderness after forty years. Their Motives for getting the Children of Israel out of the Wilderness was due to their mindset. Have a winner's mentality, so that your Motives in your journey along the Alphabet Circle will be the best one for you.

As you travel on your Alphabet Circle, your Motive is to be aware of the things you utter. I was getting a network installed in my office. The consultant I hired wanted me to learn about all the parts of this network. I felt I was too busy and did not need to know anything other than how it works. I was talking with my nineteen-year-old son and shared with him what the consultant wanted. I told my son that I did not want to learn anything new, and did not need to know how this network functioned, or its parts. Without blinking my son informed that he was shocked at my behavior as I was limiting myself by, "Putting a limit on knowledge." He stated that if that were my attitude, I would not learn much more. He challenged me that I tell myself that I was willing to learn about the network. I accepted the challenge and learned all there was to know about this network. I changed my mindset, and hence my attitude which limited me. Sometimes, we limit ourselves to new possibilities by our mindset and utterances.

(Kim & Mauborgne, 1992), published an article, *Parables of* Leadership in The Harvard Business Review. One of the stories, *The Sound of the Forest* was about a young prince who was sent to study with a Chinese master, how to become a good ruler. After returning from his first assignment, of spending a year alone in the forest, the master asked the prince to describe what he heard. He responded by giving all the sounds of the forest: the cuckoo sings, the leaves rustle, the crickets chirp, the bees buzz, and the wind whispers. After he was finished with this description, the master told him to return to the forest to listen for what more he could hear. So the prince went back to the forest and sat for several days, and nights wondering what the master was talking about. And then it happened. One morning, he heard faint sounds that he had never heard before. He returned to the master and told him "When I listened more closely, I could hear the unheard, such as the sun warming the earth, flowers opening and the sound of the grass drinking the dew" (para.7). The master nodded and said:

To hear the unheard is a necessary discipline to be a good ruler. For only when a ruler has learned to listen to the people's hearts, un-communicated feelings, pains not expressed and complaints not spoken of, can he hope to inspire confidence in the people, understand when something is wrong and meet the true needs of its citizens (para. 7).

Your Motive is to hear the unheard as you are the ruler of your journey. Those un-communicated feelings and pains not expressed are deep within, and you must be in touch with your inner self, which is your soul, to hear the unheard. Then, you can inspire confidence in yourself. You are likened unto the people in *The Sound of the Forest*. You are now in tune with all the experiences and interactions that are entering and leaving your Circle. You will have oneness between the human and soul level interactions. You must be that Prince. With deliberate Motive, you must be able to hear the unheard.

Be on your quest to live your life with Motive. Decide what is important to you on your Alphabet Circle. You should always be at peace with your choices. If you are not at peace, you must check in with your internal energy system. Don't feel obligated to participate in things that do not sit well with your soul, just because it is pleasing to another person. When you tap into the soul, the unheard is heard. Center your thoughts, and look within for the truth that is there.

Chapter 16

N is for No-Nonsense

We are packrats! We go through life keeping many things that we should discard. We hoard because we believe that we'll need "it" sometime later. This goes on not only with personal property, but also with relationships, and even jobs. It happens all along the journey. I want you to take a No-Nonsense approach to your journey, and get rid of all, and I say, ALL the things that no longer serve you. I want you to assess each interaction, relationship or job that comes along. Ask yourself, "How is this serving me? Am I getting what I need from it?" When you ask, go deep within, and connect at the soul level for the response. If the response comes back with an uncomfortable feeling, take the No-Nonsense approach! Get rid of it! Remember that this is about you. It may seem to the other participant that the interaction is fine. Don't make it about them. You need to say, as my friend Keith would say, "It does not work for me." Keith was a very decisive person. He had the quality to figure out quickly if a particular thing or situation did not work for him and hence would let it go. For Keith, it did not matter what the other participant was thinking, or feeling. As long as it did not work for him, then it was a "goner." I encourage you to be like Keith and use the No-Nonsense approach. Find peace in your decisions, and keep going on your journey. Your environment will feel much lighter. By this, I mean, it will feel like a house that has just been spring-cleaned. It feels fresh and smells clean.

Take the No-Nonsense approach to making decisions for your life goals. What makes you tick, your likes and dislikes? That is, be your own normal, and that makes you a non-normal. Normality must have context. Whose normal and for whom? You must understand that normal for you is not the same as normal for someone else. We cannot all be painted with the same brush. We are all unique individuals. So understand what you need to be doing for your journey. Understand that you may be misunderstood when you are executing what is normal for you. Just know, that you know, you are connected to your soul level, and so you are fully aware of what you should be doing. You have decoded the energy fields, and YES! You know precisely what you should be doing.

There are societal norms and individual norms. Know when you are working with each one. Do not try to fit into other people's norms. You must march to your drumbeat. Everything you needed to be your normal was given to you before you came to the planet. At times, you may be misunderstood, but that does not make you non-normal. Take a No-nonsense approach and don't be focused on standards or societal norms. Focus on the messages you are receiving from your soul bond energies. These messages are instructing you about who you are, and what you are supposed to be.

Chapter 17

O is for Obedience

Have you been paying attention? Have you been connecting the dots? Are you now in sync with the ebb, and flow of your life? If you are, you will know that those who are still on the journey with you, are supposed to be there at this point. However, that does not mean that they will accompany you to the letter Z. But for now, enjoy the lessons you're learning on your journey, whether it's from a job, a trip, or a friendship.

So, what is Obedience on your Alphabet Circle? Obedience takes place when you are aware of what your soul is reporting, and you act upon it. Thus,

Awareness with Action leads to Obedience. It happens in sequence. First, you become aware. Then, you have the opportunity to take action and be Obedient. No Obedience exists without awareness. To the contrary, you can become aware, and decide not to take action. Obedience is critical for the journey. This means you cannot be Obedient if you are not paying attention.

Awareness + Action = Obedience

Many persons who worked or had business in the World Trade Center on September 11, 2001, reported that they are alive today because they were delayed that morning for one reason or another. They were Obedient to their soul level awareness, whether consciously or unconsciously. Because they were in tune with their awareness, they missed one of worst disasters we ever experienced in the United States.

Are you Obedient to what your soul is saying to you? Are you listening to what the universe is reporting? You may decide to go to a particular place, and then you may change your mind about going. How many times has this happened to you? In other words, you change your mind because something deep inside of you tells you not to go. This something inside says, "It's just not a good day to go to that place." Suddenly, you are feeling confused because you committed in your mind to go, and now you have an impending feeling not to go. You may feel no peace about your decision, but after some time, you decide to give in to the way you are feeling, and not go. You carry on with your day, and at the end of the evening you watch the news and realize that there had been a massive pile up on the interstate highway route. It happened about the same time you would have been there. You are in awe, and thankful that you were Obedient to that feeling earlier that day. You were Obedient to your soul.

If you pay attention to your soul, you will never go wrong. But most times, we tend to think at the human level and make our decisions based on what we believe is right at the time. We ignore what our soul is reporting to us.

I mentioned earlier that the universe reports, but without Obedience, you cannot benefit from the report. Obedience is predicated on many things, such as listening, understanding, and processing information in a way that it appeals to you, to trigger action.

Chapter 18

P is for the Past & Present

The Present is all you have. You do not have the Past, as it is gone. Willingly or unwillingly, you will need to leave it behind because you actually cannot live the Past in the Present. We spend so much of our time going back, to replay events of the Past that we cannot do anything about. We relive emotions such as worry and or fear that are not beneficial to us. Why do we do this? What part of us finds it necessary to do this? We have zero control over the Past.

As humans we like to look back at the Past. However, if your focus is behind you, it is like looking in your rearview mirror while driving. When you continue to look backward, you will have a head-on collision because the car is moving forward. How can one chase the past and expect any kind result? I want you to think of it in these terms. When you focus on the Past, the space in which you are Present is just ignored, or it does not exist. However, the only thing that does exists, is the Present.

Recognize the Past is an illusion—it does not exist. We tend to spend our energy going after the Past. As a result, we get disappointed and hurt, not knowing that we are only chasing shadows.

Recently, I was talking with a friend who had lost her job. As we spoke, I could hear the pain in her voice. She believed she got fired because of a letter she had written years ago to her Human Resources department, complaining about unfair work practices.

Now, she had no proof that what she was thinking was true. But because she was living in that Past experience, she was in pain. She brought a Past experience to her Present space, connected the two without any evidence, and suffered a devastating feeling because of her thinking. Don't do this—live in the Present!

In America, during the football season, we all tend to do what is called, "Monday Morning Quarterbacking." We review the games played previously and decide what we would have done, to get a different outcome, had we been the Coach. Let's think about this. We have a game already played in its entirety. All plays have been revealed, and with this, we are trying to redo the game. Unfortunately, in football, all calls are only relevant during the game. It is about the Present, so there is no opportunity to change the result. If your team lost, no matter how you replay the game in your mind, your team result will not change to a win. You are using your "now" moment to live in the Past. So you are not available for the Present. This means, the space you're in at that moment in time is not benefitting you in the Present, because you are mentally living in the Past. You are not at your highest self.

We all have a brain that plays the tape from the records of all our experiences and events that are held in the subconscious mind. We sometimes go back to our recordings to soothe ourselves or relive Past experiences that no longer serve us well. Sometimes we go back for reference. Regardless of why we go back to the recording, it is the Past. We must remember this when we go back so that our response is with purpose, and in perspective.

In the moment of recording, we need to be Present with what is going on around us. Understand that, the Past is your mind's re-creation of what it remembers. It does not always mean it happened that way, but how you recalled it, based on your interpretation of the experience. This is one of the most significant problems with the Past. Our memories are not necessarily giving us the truth as it happened. It's giving us a re-creation of what it believed happened.

All relationships on the Alphabet Circle that are not Present are in the Past. Some can be classified as future, but they too will eventually be Present, and then Past. This is so because the future does not exist. When you get to the future, it becomes the now, which is the Present. Why do we spend so much time talking about the future, which does not exist? Is it so that we can live somewhere outside of the Present? The future is in our imagination. It is so imaginary that it's all made up in our minds. It's a projection of what we can attain. Hence, it is essential to focus on positive things instead of the negative. The universe will give you an experience according to what you project into the now. Not yesterday, not tomorrow, but now. The experience is about the now. Think of a goal post, and every time you come within a few short feet of it, it moves. You will never get to the goal. That is what the future is, a movable goal, but an attainable goal.

If you are living in the Past, you are not living in the Present. In everything you do on your journey, be Present. As you go through each day performing simple routines, such as brushing your teeth or washing your face, be Present in the moment. Be Present with the act of brushing your teeth with your toothbrush, as it moves over your teeth, massaging the gums, back and forth, side to side as it goes. This experience of being present makes it an enjoyable moment, not just something you have to do. The same goes for taking your shower or vacuuming your carpet. Your once mundane activities are now enjoyable activities because you are Present with them. In those moments when your mind drifts off, pull your mind right back to what you are doing in the Present. Take deep breaths and refocus.

During the warm months, I have a friend Isis, who I walk with four to five times per week. For some reason unknown to me, my friend is always in a hurry. She's in a hurry to get to the park where we walk. She's in a rush to complete the walk. She doesn't pause to embrace the activity and be fully Present. One day, I asked her, "What's the reason for your hurry?" She stopped and looked at me with eyes wide. She did not have an answer. I used that moment to suggest, that she would be better served if, she looked at our walk as a moment when she was doing something for herself. I continued, "If you gave yourself permission to embrace, and enjoy the moment, the time spent walking would be helpful to you becoming a better mother, a better wife, and a better friend." After a long and thoughtful pause, she thanked me for saying those words. She told me that she never saw it that way. She just felt that there was always something that she had to hurry back to do. She said, "While I am here walking in the park, it is time I use to organize my day for tomorrow and make a mental note of all the things I have to do." How many of us go through life this way? How many persons do you know who live like this in their daily lives, on their Alphabet Circle?

Let's explore this idea. The walk is three miles long on one lap; so let's say for these three miles, my friend is mentally absent from her body, which means she is Present in some other place. She was in the park with me only in her physical body. She was thinking of all the things she had to do in the future, whether it was for tomorrow or next week. The irony of is, it is impossible to organize the future because it doesn't exist. You can only act in the Present. So being absent from the Present, she still was not able to accomplish anything. Tomorrow can't be organized, because it is the future. Sometimes on your journey, you have to help someone else to S-T-O-P and B-R-E-A-T-H-E in the Present.

If you think of it, at the *soul-to-soul* interactions, the bonds formed are allowing energy to be available so that you can tap into it. When you are tapped in at the human level, this brings enjoyment to the activity you are doing in the now. Remember, there is communication always at the soul level. However, the *soul-to-soul* bonds will wait for you to act at the human level. The Past and Present principles are active anywhere or at any point on the Alphabet Circle. It does not matter which letter you are on; you must live in the Present. Let the Past go! Those Past *soul-to-soul* interactions have exited your Circle. So get the lesson from the experience while they are on the Circle with you. If you have a memory of them, you may recall them, but they are not on the journey with you anymore.

You will enjoy the best of your interactions or relationships when you are fully Present. For example, if a friend wants to share a story with you, give that friend all of your attention by being Present. What does this mean? It means that not only will your body be there, and be Present, but your mind and soul will be there as well. You are listening to all that your friend is saying, not letting your mind wander off to think about all the things you have to do later on. Don't get distracted. Park your mind, body, and soul in the Present. Immerse yourself in the experience of the story with your friend. You have the Present now. You do not have the Past. Live your life in the NOW!

Chapter 19

Q is for Quest

Why are you here? Be on a Quest to find your purpose. What is your purpose, and how do you find out?

These questions are asked a lot, and some of us have difficulty finding the right answers. In my Quest to discover my purpose, I went off to pharmacy school at the urging of my parents. Because chemistry was my favorite subject, the study of Pharmacy seemed right to me, at the time. I enjoyed all the courses in pharmacy school and learned a lot. In my final year of this program, and while completing my practicum,

I realized that my spirit did not align with the practice of pharmacy. I made a decision that I would never practice in that profession because it did not reflect my true vocation. So I went on and pursued a degree in chemistry, which I loved. In looking back at my life, I realized that my purpose for studying pharmacy was not to practice it, but to gain the knowledge I needed to pursue my Quest for the field of Chemistry, Environmental Science, and Public Health, which have become my passion.

When you are living and operating in your purpose, you will be in its flow and at peace because living in your purpose comes easily and with enjoyment.

Be on your Quest to follow your passion. Your passion is an indication of where you need to go to find your purpose on your Alphabet Circle.

While in graduate school, I met a young lady who was a medical doctor. She was a brilliant person, who had worked at the Mayo Clinic. She was pursuing a Masters in Public Health so that she could bring Occupational Health to her medical practice. We were working on a project together, so we had the opportunity to talk about our lives. One day, as we were busy trying to finalize our class project she said, "I don't even know why I am doing this." I then asked, "What do you mean?" She replied, "Long story." I suggested we take a coffee break, and we packed up our notebooks and computers and walked to the coffee shop. On our way there, my classmate shared that she had not wanted to go to medical school and only did it because her parents wanted her to go, and she felt the need to please them. Now she was feeling even more terrible because she not only completed many years of medical training, but here she was working on an additional degree program to complement her medical degree. She said that her parents had spent so much money on her education, and were now looking forward to her finishing school, and setting up her practice, which they were prepared to finance. She could do the work with ease but shared that she, "Did not enjoy any of it." In shock, I asked, "Well, what is it that you would like to do?" She said, "I want to open a daycare center." Then she continued, "I like working with children, and this is my passion. This is really what I want to do, but I will disappoint my parents." I could see the pain in her expression as she spoke to me. I suggested that she followed her heart, but I am not sure if she did or not, because after graduate school we never kept in touch. Without pursuing your Quest, for your real passion, there can be great suffering for the individual.

Be on the Quest to be obedient and connect the dots to tell your story. Connect the dots to create your picture. Your answers lie within your story or picture. Be on the Quest for your happiness as this is what makes you, you.

Part of your priority in your Quest is to look within. Look within and measure the response that you feel. Be on your Quest to resolve all issues, and be aware of unresolved matters. Have you ever been in a situation where you asked a question of someone, and the reaction of the other person was so explosive that you knew it could not have been the result of what you just said, but something more profound? You may be right because the person may have had remnants of unresolved matters that showed up when the next opportunity arose. Why is this so? The remnants are those electrons we discussed in Chapter 1. They are not stable. They must be resolved by forming bonds, whether covalent or ionic. In other words, they are seeking a resolve, so they will show up until there is a resolution. Remember, everything in this life journey must move toward a state of balance or be in balance.

Be on your Quest to acquire the desires of your heart. These are the things that you desire for you.

The universe hears those desires coming from the "energy of desire" deep within. A desire of the heart is a yearning, and the universe will respond to it.

A friend of mine wanted to have a farm. Though she lived in the city and was satisfied with her lifestyle, she yearned to have this farm. One day, while she was out visiting a friend in the countryside, she told him that she was looking to purchase farmland. The friend responded, "The owner next door to me is selling his farm." She bought the property to set up her farm. She had the desire to have this farm, and the universe responded by putting her in the presence of a friend who had the information she needed. The universe knows what you need, and delivers at the right time.

Be on your own Quest for enlightenment. The wisdom of life can be yours. There is a profound story, called *The wisdom of the Mountain* in *The Parables of Leadership,* published by (Kim & Mauborgne, 1992) in The "Harvard Business Review." This story reiterates the Quest for enlightenment. It tells of a tale in ancient China where the enlightened one dwelled in a temple on top of Mount Ping. He had many disciples. One of his disciples—Lao-Li, studied under him for twenty years, but he never gained the "wisdom of life." The story discusses that:

> Lao-li struggled with his lot for days, nights, months, even years, until one morning, the sight of a falling cherry blossom spoke to his heart. "I can no longer fight my destiny," he reflected. "Like the cherry blossom, I must gracefully resign myself to my lot." From that moment forth, Lao-Li determined to retreat down the mountain, giving up his hope of enlightenment. Lao-li then went in search of his master Hwan to tell him of his decision. The master sat before a white wall, deep in meditation.

Reverently, Lao-li approached him. "Enlightened one," he said. But before he could continue, the master spoke, "Tomorrow I will join you on your journey down the mountain." No more needed to be said. The great master understood. The next morning, before their descent, the master looked out into the vastness surrounding the mountain peak and said, "Tell me, Lao-li what do you see?" Lao-li responded, "Master, I see the sun beginning to wake just below the horizon, meandering hills and mountains that go on for miles, and couched in the valley below, a lake and an old town." The master listened to Lao-Li's response. He smiled, and then they took the first steps of their long descent. Hour after hour, as the sun crossed the sky, they pursued their journey, stopping only once as they approached the foot of the mountain. Again, Hwan asked Lao-li to tell him what he saw. Lao-li responded, "Great wise one, in the distance I see roosters as they run around barns, cows asleep in sprouting meadows, old ones basking in the late afternoon sun, and children romping by a brook." The master, remaining silent, continued to walk until they reached the gate to the town. There the master gestured to Lao-li, and together they sat under an old tree. "What did you learn today, Lao-li?" asked the master. Then he continued, "Perhaps this is the last wisdom I will impart to you." Silence, was Lao-li's response. At last, after long silence, the master said. "The road to enlightenment is like the journey down the mountain. It comes only to those who realize that what one sees at the top of the mountain is not what one sees at the bottom" (para. 25).

Without this wisdom, we close our minds to all that we cannot view from our position, and so we limit our capacity to grow and improve. However, with this wisdom, there comes an awakening. This is the wisdom that opens our minds to improvement, knocks down prejudices, and teaches us to respect what at first we cannot view.

Know that your vantage point is vital for enlightenment. Enlightenment is coming to the realization that you are. Be on your Quest to find enlightenment and happiness in all your relationships and interactions. Be on your Quest to create the life you want. Be deliberate and methodical. This will always be liberating for you. All you are enjoying, is life unfolding.

Chapter 20

R is for River

How does soul interaction manifest on your Alphabet Circle? How is it demonstrated in your journey? Let's take a look at what we are attracting in our lives.

Check yourself by looking within. Manifestations are reflected at the human level. Through all of this, you have the power to create the things you desire. You also have the power to change the things you don't like. But to assess your actions and feelings, you must look within. At the soul level, is the truth. But this truth is not forced upon you as you have free will to make your choices. You, however, have the opportunity to tap into that truth at any time. When you are connected to this truth, you are in your purest form. You could climb Mt. Everest! At this place, every goal is attainable and achievable. This is where you get the desires of your heart because you are connected to a River flowing with enlightenment, awareness, and consciousness. As long as you are tapped in, the flow continues. Disconnect, and it disrupts the flow. So you see, it is important to have your mind in the right place at all times so that your creativity can be at its highest level. I believe this is self-actualization. This is the true self.

A River is a natural stream of water that flows throughout the land and empties itself into a body of water, an ocean or lake. Paul, one of the scholars of the Bible writes, "Be sober, be alert and cautious at all times" (1st Peter 5:8, Amplified Bible). This is what sobriety is about. It is about being present. It is about being aware and conscious because it is only in this space that you can create at your highest level. This is where you can connect to the River of truth, and its contents.

Imagine, a River with voluminous amounts of water carrying colliding rocks as it makes its way to the eventual ocean. The contents are colliding because they are bumping into each other, and the riverbed. This is the same with the stuff you carry on your Alphabet Circle. They are colliding with each other at all times. As the rocks, pebbles, and debris collide, the total noise depends on the volume of water; the lessor the volume, the higher the decibels, the louder the sound. So is your connection to your true self. When you are not sufficiently connected to your true self, there is a lot of background noise, just like what's going on in the Riverbed. You have a lot of distraction because your River volume is low. You are not fully connected, and thus not committed to the connection. The rocks and pebbles in your life are rolling along at very high decibels. The sounds are very audible to you at the human level, drowning out everything that is happening around you. The sounds can manifest as noises in your head. They can be audible to other folks on your Circle, and manifest in your demeanor. They can also be other things in your life that you carry along your Circle.

Just as the River ends in the ocean, where it gets rid of its contents, the same is true for the soul. Your ocean can be at any letter on the Alphabet Circle. Therefore, it can be very close, or it can be far away. Once you establish your connection to this River of truth and the volume is right, the contents are allowed to flow until, the River ends. Your River's end is where you resolve your issues or matters on the Alphabet Circle. You can get rid of these issues by looking within, and making a *soul-to-soul* connection that supports awareness, consciousness, and enlightenment.

This River serves as a cleansing agent for both you and your journey. It gets rid of negative things in your life. It gets rid of things that no longer serve you. Cleansing your mind of old relationships and patterns are essential so that you are always in your purest form. It can be cleansing of the mind as well as cleansing of the body. Cleansing is removing the dead cells from your life so that you can shine, and it brings forth a new perspective.

Chapter 21

S is for Soul

You and only you, have a window to your Soul. You and you only have a connection to your Soul.

The Soul is your thermostat.

The Soul is your thermometer.

The Soul is your media.

The Soul is your gut feeling.

The Soul is "my mind told me."

The Soul is "my spirit told me."

The Soul knows only love.

The Soul is centering.

The Soul is not judgmental.

The Soul leads towards balance.

The Soul is your clock.

The Soul is your sunlight.

The Soul is your playground.

The Soul is your social media.

The Soul is your Google and your search engine.

The Soul is your reference library.

The Soul is your source.

The Soul is your radar.

The Soul is your GPS.

The Soul is your flashlight.

The Soul is your school.

The Soul is your telegraph. It is never wrong. It is that which created you in this life. It is your guiding light. It's embedded with all the answers you need. Your Soul is where you go to find solutions to any questions, you may have. Just as in life, if you want to know the temperature, you check with your thermometer; the Soul is your meter, which I will call the Soul-meter. It will let you know the temperature of an interaction or relationship, if you choose to consult it. Remember, just like any other meter; you must check it, to get the answer.

You may ask, "How do I let this Soul-meter work for me?" It is a simple process. First, you always want to remember that you need to check in with your Soul to find the answers you are seeking. To do this, you look deep inside—close your eyes, get quiet, and observe what you feel. This is your gut feeling. Sometimes, at the human level, you may not agree with the gut feeling, because you think you want something other than what the Soul-meter is delivering to you, at that moment. Double check to make sure the feeling is the same feeling you had before. If you can't decide upon the feeling you are getting, make no decision. This means you did not understand what the Soul reported, which might be for many reasons. It could be that the answer is not what you want to hear or feel at that moment. It may be that there is just too much noise in the environment, and the correct signal and the energy are drowned out. It may also be that you are just not paying attention.

In many situations in life people will tell you that they are going to pray about something or that they "will pray on a particular situation." They mean that they will wait to feel peace about the decision or situation. When the Soul reports and you are tapped into its energy, you have an awakening and peace. The peace comes when the human level and Soul level energies are in alignment. If we went through life or traveled on our journey listening and responding to the Soul, we would only make good decisions. We will not make bad decisions if we learn to pay attention to the guidance. Know that the response of the Soul is offered to give you the answers. It is not forced upon you, so you may choose to accept it or not. However, know that in rejecting it, you are setting yourself up for the ramifications of not making the right decisions. And then you might say to yourself, "If I had only known."

The Soul will never lead you astray. It will signal when you are in challenging situations. It will provide signals for you when you come upon interactions that you should give more attention. It will also signal you when you come upon right situations. Remember, the Soul is your gauge. Pay attention to the Soul energy that is rising from deep within you.

The Soul knows all things. The Soul sees all things. This must be so for the Soul to guide you. What a precious thing it is. It is your pilot on the aircraft of life, Soul Airways, destined to fly on the Alphabet Circle. The path is one-directional, and it only goes forward. It is flying toward the letter Z, making as many stops as necessary to get there. You are on a flight with many stops, and many connections as needed to get you to your destination. Fasten your seatbelt, and get ready for takeoff. The Soul will do the rest of the work.

Chapter 22

T is for Tolerance

Tolerance is your test on the Alphabet Circle. Tolerance is a goal to be achieved. However, there are so many other things you have to embrace before you can become Tolerant. First, you have to be present. Second, you cannot take anything personally. Third, you cannot judge, and fourth, you must forgive. If you do these four things, you will become Tolerant.

Understand that Tolerance will alleviate frustrations for you on your Alphabet Circle journey. My friend Ana, told me that the folks she worked for had no morals. After further conversation, I learned that the statement was made because of her idea of morals. I explained to Ana that she could not use her morals to judge other people. They had different life experiences and were looking through different lenses. However, it does not make them immoral. Both parties were not seeing things the same way. Know that, on this life journey, you are going to meet people who do not see things the same way you do, and that is okay. We are all unique individuals, and we have all had different experiences that define us on our Alphabet Circle journey. When you practice Tolerance, you are not judging. Practicing Tolerance here means, you are aware that someone else is seeing the same thing but from a different perspective, which does not make him or her a bad person, nor does it make him or her wrong.

Tolerance comes when you are tapped into your *soul-to-soul* bond, and you are attuned. You are fully present with the energy from the *soul-to-soul* bond. Practicing Tolerance means, you are willing to accept when your *soul-to-soul* bonds break, and your relationships end. In this mode, you do not question. You recognize that the universe gives you the experience you need at the moment, and stop it, when it's appropriate.

When you understand that we are all unique individuals, your Tolerance level will be elevated. When you know that we all think differently, and see things differently, your Tolerance level will be raised. When you become aware that you are defining yourself in every experience, you will operate in that experience until you learn the lesson you need to learn. This is Tolerance.

Tolerance understands that there is no need to be right or wrong. It just is. The Alphabet Circle is about embracing Tolerance and understanding that there will be many points of views, and rightfully so. No one on this journey should be boxed into a particular thought or feeling. It is a free-spirited journey, if you are living it in your higher self

Chapter 23

U is for Universe

Your Alphabet Circle is your Universe. It is your world. It is your life. It is your creation. It is a place in which you work, play, and thrive. This earth is a part of your Universe. What does the Universe represent to us? It represents completion. The Universe provides the additional things you need to excel on your journey. Everything on your Alphabet Circle journey has a place in the Universe. The Universe gives that space to complete your picture. Many things are in the Universe, and they exist together in unison, and each one minding its own business and doing its job. So it is in the Universe of your Alphabet Circle journey. Everything on the Alphabet Circle can thrive together in harmony. Each one knows its assignment and carries it out.

Just as the Universe is a vast span, and within it are light, darkness, the sun, the moon, and the stars. So it is on your Alphabet Circle journey. You have all you need for your journey. However, you must know how to "make hay while the sun shines." For example, if you will need sunlight to perform a task and you choose to perform the task at night when there is no sunlight, the result cannot be maximized. Know that some opportunities show up on your Alphabet Circle journey, and if you do not make the right choice, you might end up on a path that is not conducive to the experience you may need at the time. To avoid this, check in with your soul level to ensure that you have a "good sense" or feeling about your choice. Yes, on your Alphabet Circle journey, in your Universe, you and only you have the power to choose. This means you can choose the path of least resistance, which is your best path. Stay connected to both your human and soul level connections. Focus on interpreting the energy fields around you, and read all the signs along the way. Now, follow the messages you have been given.

Know that if the rain is pouring down, and you walk in it without an umbrella or raincoat, you will get wet. Know the right attire or gear to shift into for the proper occasions on your Alphabet Circle. If you choose the wrong attire, you will be soaking wet. Being wet can have further consequences. You could get sick, you could get a cold, and you could get pneumonia. Be aware of the conditions in your Universe, which is your journey. Know how to deal with any change, and have the right tools to overcome the conditions on your journey.

Chapter 24

V is for Veracity

The truth is, you belong here at this time. The Veracity of your authenticity is that, where you are on your Alphabet Circle is where you belong at that time. When you know this, you will have a sense of presence. Knowing this brings a feeling of peace over you. An example that comes to mind that strikes me most is, when I return to my native homeland, Jamaica. As soon as the airplane gets over Cuba, I know I am not far away from my native land, and I get excited. It doesn't matter how many times I've made this trip; I still get excited about going. As soon as the landing gear goes down, and the wheels of the airplane touch the ground of Sangster International Airport, my heart jumps for joy, and a certain peace comes over me. I would refer to this feeling as the "the peace that passeth all understanding." As soon as I disembark and my feet hit the ground, my mind knows that I am on my native soil, and a secure feeling comes over me. This feeling is that "I belong here." This feeling tells me, I fit into this place, and no one can dare to say, I don't belong here. This is the kind of peace I feel when I return to my homeland.

Let's find out what you are supposed to be doing now that you know you are supposed to be here? When you have a sense of "belonging," you exist with a great sense of security. You can form great friendships. You can focus on who you are at the core of your being, because you feel that your surroundings pose no threat to you. You carry very little or manageable baggage that will impact your interactions in a negative way.

You walk with your shoulders back, and your head held high because you know. Yes! You know that you know, that you belong here. And, so you can understand that if you accept this, and you accept the Veracity that all the experiences you've had, and will have are what you need at the time.

Embrace your journey. Show up and be present. You deserve to be here. Knowing that you belong is indeed not enough for a peaceful journey. You must now do. You must now tap into your river flow, be always present, aware, and conscious.

What is indeed the Veracity of your journey? Let's step back and figure it out. There are so many things that we think are true, or that it happened, but it did not. If we stop to pay attention to our thoughts, we will realize that they are thoughts. Our thoughts are not who we are. Somehow, we tend to believe that our thoughts are who we are. Be true to every moment on your Alphabet Circle journey.

What is true about your journey? It is indeed your journey. Back in time when you were just spirit, your soul created a journey for you, and this is why you are here. It is no accident that you came. In the story of the Creation, I have never read or heard anywhere that the Creator came back to the earth to do maintenance, or tweak His Creation. Let's think about this for a minute. The Creation is very profound! The Book of Genesis describes the event in great detail, and nowhere in it, tells of the Creator "going back, correcting and measuring." There is no report of continuous improvement. There is no report of quality control. So, what does this mean? There was no need for a quality control program. The Creation was perfect! So it is for you. You were made perfect for your journey on your Alphabet Circle. You came to the earth equipped with everything that you need for your journey. You came perfectly adequate! There is no need for correcting and measuring and tweaking as far as you go. This is your Veracity. Knowing this, I want you to dig deep. Reach deep within, and pull out the tools you need for greater understanding on this journey. They are within you. This is your Veracity. You have no deficiency. This is your Veracity. It is not what you ultimately look like, or believe are the circumstances of your life on this journey, but learning to change the outcome and how you accept whatever it is that you are not happy with within yourself. It is the acceptance of it that will make the change in you. You are perfect for your journey. This is your Veracity.

So as you embark upon and embrace your journey; know that it is the right journey for you. King David writes in the Psalms, "The steps of a good man are ordered" (Psalm 37:23, New King James Version). Know that your steps have been ordered on your journey. Embrace all the support you have been provided with along your Alphabet Circle, as they are supposed to be there. They are there for you to learn the lessons you need on your journey. The lessons are:

To lift you up when needed

To catch you when you fall

To listen when you need an ear

To provide food for your journey

To be a blessing

This is your Veracity.

Chapter 25

W is for Window

A Window gives a view to something. A Window provides some picture or scenery for the eyes to see. Which Window are you looking through? What is the scenery that is beyond the view of the Window? What you see may be different from what another person sees through that same Window. Know that we all look out of different Windows, and what we see depends on our experiences, and our context. The sun may be shining in your Window, but it does not mean that it is not raining in someone else's Window. So, on this Alphabet Circle journey, the questions you will always need to ask yourself in your interactions are, "Are they seeing things through my Window? Do they see things from my vantage point? Do they understand my view through the Window?"

Everybody's picture in his or her Window is how he or she perceives life. Your experiences and environment contribute to your perception also. I want to tell you that your perception is your reality. For the person who is the perceiver, that person believes what he or she is experiencing is real. And yes! For them it is real. It is the perceiver's reality. If we take the concept of the Johari Window (The Institute for Motivational Living, Inc., 2011), we know that there are always things that the perceiver is seeing that others don't see, and vice versa. How do we relate the Johari Window to the concept of the Alphabet Circle? Well, the Johari Window consist of four Windows, the first is the Arena, which is open communication. Here there is common knowledge. What you are viewing through the Arena space others are also viewing. Therefore, all have the same information. Everyone can see the information in the Window. However, it does not mean that the interpretations will be the same for everyone. Next, there is the Mask or Hidden Window. The view from this Window is hidden from others. Only you are able to see what's inside this Window. You must remember this, if you find yourself in this Window; you are the only one that have the information. Remember, no one else is seeing or experiencing what you are seeing from this Window. From the vantage point of this Window on the Alphabet Circle, you may be misunderstood because you are the only one looking at the information. Then, there is the Blind Spot, also called Self-discovery. In this Window, others will see and experience things you will not. In this space, there can be disagreements due to the nature of the Window. If you find yourself in this Window on the Alphabet Circle, remember that it is about self-discovery. You will find out things about yourself that others will not know. The fourth Window is the Potential, also known as the Unknown. In this Window, you do not know, neither do others know what is there—no one knows. If you find yourself in the Potential Window, just remember that it is unknown for all parties. You do not have the information and neither does anyone else looking through that Window.

So, along the path of the Alphabet Circle, you need to always move toward the Arena. This is where your interactions will be at maximum because of trust. You and others will know, and see the same things through the same Arena Window. Consequently, you will all be on the same page at the same time. But will the interpretations be the same? No, each person brings a different experience to the Window and thus, a different understanding. Your take away from your perspective of the Johari Window experience will dictate how you interpret your world.

Windows of opportunities also exist on your Alphabet Circle. Know when these opportunities present themselves. When they are present, it is time to seize the moment. The presented opportunity may never show up again. Know when you are at this Window on your Alphabet Circle. The Windows of your souls are reporting.

Chapter 26

X is for X-ray

The X-ray process can be described as, "To expose something, such as a part of the body to X-rays to obtain a photographic image of it" (Google). Just as your X-ray shows on a film so does your Alphabet Circle journey. It is captured and recorded. The X-ray is for the revelation of the inside of your body. Let's say, it reveals hard tissues, and your soul reveals soft tissue. Therefore, for a complete picture of inside your Alphabet Circle, you need to interpret *soul-to-soul* bonds and X-rays.

You can think of your journey as a camera that takes pictures. But in the case of the Alphabet Circle, every interaction or relationship is captured on film. As with an X-ray film, you can view your Alphabet Circle journey "down to the bone." You can create a film that will energize you upon review.

An X-ray is a picture of the inside of someone's body. Your Alphabet Circle journey X-ray will also capture all your energy levels. On this film, you will see the energies of other souls as they enter the Circle, when they form bonds, and when they exit the Circle. Your happy energy is on this film. How does it look to you? Your unhappy energy is also on this film. How does it seem to you? Your Impact map as we discussed earlier, is also captured on the film of your Alphabet Circle. How does it look? Your entire journey is also recorded on this film. Are you excited about this X-ray film?

You are looking at this film, and you can see every "nook and cranny" of your Alphabet Circle journey. Now that you understand all the events are recorded on X-ray, how are you prepared to live your journey?

There are items such as aluminum foil that will block X-rays. Some of the interactions or relationships are an aluminum foil on your Alphabet Circle journey. Pay attention to unwrap these foils, so that whatever is deep inside can be revealed. When you cross the security checkpoint at the airport, the authorities want to make sure, you are not carrying anything that is dangerous to yourself, or others, on your person, or in your carry-on luggage. This is precisely how you have to view your Alphabet Circle journey. You want to see what is going on inside the Circle that could be dangerous to you or anyone else, and gladly remove these items or behaviors from your Alphabet Circle. These items could be disguised as friends wrapped in aluminum foil. These items will also block your flow of energy. Get rid of them.

Chapter 27

Y is for Yes

Yes! Say it loudly. Yes! Say it clearly. Yes! I'm on the Alphabet Circle journey. Yes! I'm committed to doing my part. Yes! I'll create great relationships. Yes! I am the author of my destiny. Yes! I am responsible for my success. Yes! I am accountable for my failures. There are many Yeses on this, your Alphabet Circle. Say them aloud.

Yes! I am on my life's journey.

Yes! I am the author of my universe.

Yes! I am the author of my story.

Yes! I will pay attention.

Yes! I will Breathe.

Yes! I will endure.

Yes! I will Create.

Yes! I will remove weeds from my Alphabet Circle.

Yes! I will live in the ebb and flow.

Yes! I will look within.

Yes! I will connect to my River.

Yes! My relationships are Finite.

Yes! I will know my location at all times.

Yes! I will choose to find my Happiness balance.

Yes! I will have an Impact.

Yes! I will make the right choices.

Yes! I am King of my kingdom.

Yes! I will have laughter on my Alphabet Circle journey.

Yes! I will live with Motive.

Yes! I will connect the dots.

Yes! I will live in the Present.

Yes! I will choose not live in the Past.

Yes! I will find my life's purpose.

Yes! I will be resolute.

Yes! I am responsible for my happiness.

Yes! I am committed to this journey.

Yes! I'm supposed to be here.

Yes! I will live the theory of the sunflower seed!

Yes! I will review my X-rays.

Yes! I am on my Eureka.

Chapter 28

Z is for Zealous

Z is the last letter of the alphabet, and it represents the end phase of your Alphabet Circle journey. The relationships that are here with you have been tried and tested. You are now experienced at this stage of your Alphabet Circle journey. Life, as you know it, "has happened." It has probably dealt its blows. But here you are! You have come out shining on the other side. This is a reflective stage. You are now able to look back at your journey and make decisions as to what you thought it was about, and what it meant for you. Here, you have had the opportunity to put things in perspective. Here, you can exercise quality control measures. You can correct and measure all interactions. You are on your way out. But you do want to go out with a bang! That is, enjoying your most significant interactions.

You are now intense about your experiences. It is all coming together. The pieces of the puzzle are being filled in. I learned in High School that Archimedes, a great scientist was in his bathtub when he discovered the "Principle of Upthrust." He ran into the streets shouting, "Eureka! Eureka!" Translated, I have found it! You must now shout your own Eureka. And then you would say, "I am here in my Eureka! And I feel good!"

You now understand the human relationship with the soul relationship. You soon realize that everything on the Alphabet Circle journey is finite, and it has an end date. Don't sweat the small stuff. You are about to or have closed all the chapters on your Alphabet Circle journey. Some interactions are indelibly printed on your mind, and some are not. You feel great, knowing that you have carried with you, the tools necessary to guide you along your journey. These tools have made your journey more comprehensible.

In this phase of your journey, you fully understand "The Theory of the Sunflower Seed," which is maximizing resources while multiplying. A sunflower seed when planted and nurtured grows into a tree that bears one flower. As this flower grows, she points her face towards the sunlight. As she gets bigger and more beautiful, her petals open wide, exposing thousands of seeds. As it matures, her flower turns downward away from the sun, and become even more attractive. The one seed produces a flower, bearing thousands of seeds. So it is on your Alphabet Circle journey. It takes one idea, to be nurtured and cared for, to blossom into a product, a service, or an empire.

Be Zealous as the sunflower on your Alphabet Circle journey.

Souls are on the last phase of their interactions or relationships. They are winding down and preparing to exit when that time comes, and it will be soon enough. *Soul-to-soul* communications are intense, as they know this is the last phase. They show up and are present. You have been devoted, and you have been diligent. Yes! You have been Zealous.

Chapter 29

The Lights come on—The Ah Ha Moment

We now know that, all relationships or interactions on your Alphabet Circle journey are Finite. Souls come together because of soul chemistry, which is based on a want or a need. When souls come together, they form bonds. When souls exit the Alphabet Circle, they break these bonds. Soul energy is released from the forming or breaking of bonds. The released energy contains coded information for you the host. Decode this information, and you are on your way to your "perfect" journey. From all your interactions on the Alphabet Circle, there are Impacts. Learn to connect all your Impact dots to create your Impact map.

So how do we move forward on our Circle to live each day with a sense of peace, and purpose? How do we look within and use our energy to uplift ourselves, regardless of our situations? We now know that we need to be **Alright** in our space by accepting the beginning and end of every interaction because of the required experience. From every experience, lessons are learned. Embrace every experience as though it's your last.

We now know to **Breathe** as we move through our space, and enjoy the relationships we encounter regardless of what it brings. Know that you are where you are supposed to be because there are lessons to be learned. You are equipped for every situation on your Alphabet Circle journey if you pay attention. It can be an enjoyable journey. **B**elieve **R**elationships **E**nter the **A**lphabet **C**ircle **T**o **H**elp you **E**ndure. **Breathe** and look within before you react to each situation. Sometimes an immediate answer is not what is needed.

Create the journey that you want to have. You are the author of your world. You are the creator of your success. You are the creator of your failures. With this in mind, **Create** exactly what you want in your journey. You have the responsibility for your own life. It is never too late to take action. So no matter where you are on your Alphabet Circle journey, you may start to **Create** the experience you want.

Pay attention to the **Details** all along the path of your life journey. The **Details** are essential on this journey. Why is this so vital? The universe is reporting all around you. It gives you all the information you need to live your desired life. The universe is your CNN, ABC or NBC providing 24hours, seven days per week coverage. Tune in to your Alphabet Circle journey, just as you would tune into your regular news stations. You will learn a lot. Listen for breaking news. Never turn your dial off. Know the right number for each channel. Otherwise, you will be listening or watching the wrong station and will be off on your Alphabet Circle journey.

The Alphabet Circle journey is your **Earth**, where your ideas and relationships will flourish. It is your playground. Be resilient and strong. Forces are waiting to rock your world at all times. Don't get capsized. Remember, this path is your playground, and you are intimately connected to it. You belong on this journey. It's your journey. Know how to recover from your **Earth** rocking moments. Seek the right help you need, if and when, you need it. Pay attention to your symptoms or "sickness," and find the right specialist to help you. Know when you need a physical doctor, a mental doctor, or a spiritual doctor. The **Earth** offers a lot of things including healing properties. Know how to get to these resources and apply them.

Remember, all interactions on the Alphabet Circle journey are **Finite**. Therefore bask in all of them. You are on your Alphabet Circle for a **Finite** period, and so is everyone else. Don't be fearful about this.

Know your **Geography** at all times. This means, know where you are and know your location. Use your human GPS; it will work well for you. Learn to identify the best path for your Alphabet Circle journey.

Be **Happy**. Decide to be **Happy** and live as such. Be deliberate with your Happiness, and stick to it, even if you fall off track momentarily. Commit to being **Happy**. It will change your life!

Review your **Impact** map, and assess the Impact of your interactions on your Alphabet Circle journey. Be satisfied with the shape and contents of your map.

You are the **Jockey** on this race. Know your horse, and ride a strategic race to bring your horse home unhurt.

Know that you are **King** or Queen of your Alphabet Circle. As **King**, you are the leader of your Alphabet Circle journey. Embrace it and let the kingship work for you.

Live on your Alphabet Circle journey with **Love**. Show **Love**, teach **Love** and preach **Love**. **Love** conquers all.

As you live, do so with the right **Motive** on your Alphabet Circle journey. Know that there are two sets of normal at play. There is societal normal and individual normal. Know which one you are working with. Your normal is when you march to your drumbeat.

Take a **No-nonsense** approach to being authentic on your Alphabet Circle journey. Rid your life of all things that no longer serve you well.

Be aware and take action to be **Obedient** on your Alphabet Circle journey. **Obedience** will open your receptivity faucets on your journey.

Remember to be **Present** at all times, and do not live in the **Past**. The universe will deliver for you as you live in the **Present**.

Make it your **Quest** to tap into the flow of your **River** of truth, so you can be wise on this your Alphabet Circle journey, to become the recipient of all good things. Tap in to be cleansed and have a new perspective.

Pay attention to your *soul-to-soul* bonds. You have the only view of your **Soul**. You are the only connection to your **Soul**. Remember, it is your internal radar, your tour guide on this your Alphabet Circle journey. Connect to it, and pay attention. Your journey will be a lot smoother. Remain present and don't take anything personally. Discipline yourself, and do not judge. Forgive.

Tolerance is a goal to achieve. Be Tolerant on this your Alphabet Circle journey. It will alleviate any frustrations that may arise.

Your Alphabet Circle journey is your **Universe**. It represents completion.

The **Veracity** of your authenticity is that where you are on your Alphabet Circle journey is where you belong at that time. Know this and enjoy all the fruits of your journey.

On this your Alphabet Circle journey, everyone has a view of a **Window**. What you see through your **Window** depends on the context of your experiences. Know this, and you will understand why you and others can look at the same **Window** and report different truths.

The Alphabet Circle journey produces **X-rays**, which can be viewed by the host. Create an **X-ray** film that you will be excited about upon review. Remove things or situations that compound your journey.

Practice, rehearse, and reinforce your **Yeses**. Say them loudly and assuredly. Repeat them until they become parts of you. **Yes**! You belong on this Alphabet Circle and, **Yes**! You are the author of your journey. **Yes**! You have been devoted and diligent. **Yes**!

You have been **Zealou**s! Now, go and live your best life on your Alphabet Circle journey.

Works Cited

Bullard, S. (2012, November 10). *Mindbodygreen.* Retrieved May 26, 2018, from How to know You've Found Your Soul Mate: Http://www.mindbodygreen.com/0-6779/How-to-Know-You've-FoundYour-Soul-Mate.html

Diener, E., & Biswas-Diener, R. (2008). *Happiness: Unlocking the Mysteries of psychological Wealth.* Malden, MA, USA: Blackwell Publishing.

Gibran, K. (1923). *The Prophet.* New York, New York, USA: Alfred A. Knopf.

Google. (n.d.). Retrieved May 20, 2018, from Google online english dictionary: Http://www.google.com/

Khoddam, R. (n.d.). *What's Your Definition of Happiness.* Retrieved May 19, 2018, from Psychology today: http://www.psychologytoday.com/us/blog/the-addition-connection/201506/whats-your-definition-of-happiness

Kim, W. C., & Mauborgne, R. (1992, July 01). *Parables of Leadership.* Retrieved May 26, 2018, from Havard Business Review: http:///www.hbr.org/1992/parables-of-leadership

Michelli, J. A. (1998). Humor Play and Laughter: Stress Proofing life with your kids. 88.

Milton, J. (1991). *Paradise Lost* (Vol. #20). USA: Project Gutenberg.

Schucman, H. (2012). *A Course in Miracles* (Original ed.). Guildford, United Kingdom: WhiteCrow Books.

Seligman, M. E. (2002). *Authentic Happiness: Using the new positive psychology to realize your potential for lasting fulfillment.* New York, New York: The Free Press.

Sheldrake, R. (2005, March). *Listen to the Animals: Why did so many animals escape December's tsunami?* Retrieved April 24, 2018, from Rupert Sheldrake: https//sheldrake.org/reaearch/animals-powers/listen-to-the-animals

The Institute for Motivational Living, Inc. (2011). Introduction to Behavioral Analysis. *Your Guide to Understanding Why People Do What They Do.* Boardman, OH, USA: Institute for Motivational Living, Inc.

Printed and bound by PG in the USA

USA2018PG1L